The
Complete Illustrated
Kama Sutra

The
Complete Illustrated
Kama Sutra

EDITED BY LANCE DANE

INNER TRADITIONS
Rochester, Vermont

Inner Traditions
One Park Street
Rochester, Vermont 05767
www.InnerTraditions.com

Text and photographs by Lance Dane

Library of Congress Cataloging-in-Publication Data
Vatsyayana.
[Kamasutra. English]
The complete illustrated Kama Sutra / edited by Lance Dane.
p. cm.
ISBN 13: 978-089281138-0
10: 0-89281138-2 (cloth)
1. Sex. 2. Love. 3. Sexual intercourse. 4. Erotic literature, Indic.
5. Erotic art-India. I. Dane, Lance. II. Title.

HQ470.S3V3 2003
613.9'6-dc21
2003051090

10 9 8 7

Text design and layout by Utsav Bhattacharya
This book was produced by Brijbasi Art Press Ltd.

Captions: (Page 1) The exuberant Rajput prince embraces his beloved and plays with her feet. (Pages 2-3) Shiva and Parvati share affectionate moments as their sons Ganesh, the elephant god and Kartikeya are engrossed in their own activities and the tiger and Nandi, the bull laze around. (Page 5) A young nayika *waits anxiously and yearns for her lover. (Pages 6-7) The amazingly attractive* nayika *in a flowing skirt stretches one leg out and places the other on her lover's shoulder, then switches positions and continues to do so alternately in a posture described as splitting of a bamboo.*

Contents

Book 4 — The Wife

Book 5 — Seducing the Wives of Others

Book 6 — The Courtesan

Book 7 — Secret Lore, Extraneous Stimulation, and Sexual Power

Preface

Every country's literature has among its treasures of the written word a number of works dealing especially with love. Everywhere too, the subject is dealt with in a different manner and from various points of view. This book is a comprehensive translation of the most authoritative work on love in Sanskrit literature - the *Kama Sutra, Aphorisms on Love* by Vatsyayana.

Divided into seven books and thirty-six parts, the evidence concerning the date of the writing and the commentaries written on it are examined in the Introduction. Before commencing the translation in the books, however, a brief mention is made about similar works written by authors who wrote years after Vatsyayana, but who still quoted him as the chief guide to Hindu erotic literature.

Rati Devi, wife of Kama takes aim with her arrow of love. Such wood sculpture was used for decorative purposes in temple rathas, chariots. (Left) Mallinaga Vatsyayana lived sometime between the first and the sixth century A.D. in Benares and led the life of a religious student.

RATIRAHASYA *(Secrets of Love)* by Kokkoka

Kokokka, a poet, composed the *Ratirahasya* to please someone called Venudutta, who was perhaps a king. Writing his own name at the end of each part of the book, he addressed himself as *siddha patiya pandita* - an ingenious man among learned men. His work was translated into Hindi long ago, and in the translation, he was referred to as Koka. With this abbreviated form of his name replacing his full name in other languages in India, the book and the subject began to be popularly called *Koka Shastra,* Doctrines of Koka, which is identical with the *Kama Shastra,* Doctrines of Love.

The *Ratirahasya* comprises nearly eight hundred verses, and is divided into fifteen parts called *Pachivedas.* Some of the subjects dealt with in this work are not to be found in Vatsyayana's translation, such as the four classes of women: the *padmini, chitrini, shankhini* and *hastini;* as also the enumeration of the days and hours on which the women of different classes were stimulated towards love. Kokkoka claimed that his knowledge of these subjects was garnered from the wisdom of Gonikaputra and Nandikesvara, both of whom have been mentioned by Vatsyayana, but whose works are not now extant. It is difficult to fix a date or year in which the *Ratirahasya* was composed. It can, however, be safely presumed that it was written after Vatsyayana's tome, and was prior to other works on the subject that are still extant. Vatsyayana, himself, referred to ten

Nandi, bull companion of lord Shiva is said to be the first formulator of the Kama Shastras or rules of love that had one thousand chapters. (Right) Shiva, is one of the major gods of the Hindu pantheon and forms with Brahma and Vishnu the great triad of Hindu deities.

authors whose work on the subject he had consulted, but none of which is extant, and Kokkoka's name does not figure among them. This leads to the logical conclusion that Kokkoka wrote after Vatsyayana, else, Vatsyayana would surely have made mention of him with the others he referred to.

PANCHASAYAKA (Five Arrows) by Jyotirisvara

Jyotirisvara, the author of *Panchasayaka,* was the most celebrated poet, the keeper of the treasure of the sixty-four arts, and the best teacher of the rules of music. He said that he composed the *Panchasayaka* after reflecting upon the aphorisms of love as revealed by the gods, and studying the opinions of Gonikaputra, Muladeva, Babhravya, Ramtideva, Nandikesvara and Kshemendra. None of these appear to be in existence now. His work contains nearly six hundred verses, divided into five parts called sayakas, or arrows.

SMARAPRADIPIKA (Light of Love) by Gunakara

The author of the *Smarapradipika* was the poet Gunakara, the son of Vachaspati. His work comprised four hundred verses and dealt only briefly with the doctrines of love, dwelling more on other matters.

RATIMANJARI (Garland of Love) by Jayadeva

The work of the poet Jayadeva, *Ratimanjari* is very short, containing only one hundred and twenty-five verses, written in an elegant style, probably in the fifteenth century.

RASAMANJARI (Sprout of Love) by Bhanudatta

The author of *Rasamanjari* was a poet called Bhanudatta. The last verse of the manuscript indicated that he was a resident of the province of Tirhoot, and son of a Brahman named Ganeshwar, who was also a poet. Written in Sanskrit, it portrays different classes of men and women through their age, description, conduct and behavior. Comprising three chapters, it has not been possible to ascertain its date.

ANANGA RANGA *(Stage of Love)* by Kalyanamalla

Ananga Ranga was composed by the poet Kalyanamalla, for the amusement of Ladkhan, the son of Ahmed Lidi. Ladkhan was also known as Ladana Mull and Ladanaballa. He was supposedly a relation of or had a connection with the house of Lodi, which reigned in India from A.D. 1450 to 1526. The work would, therefore, have been written in the fifteenth or sixteenth century. Containing ten chapters, it was translated into English but only six copies were printed for private circulation. Popularly believed to be the latest of the Sanskrit works on the subject, the ideas in it were evidently taken from previous writings of the same nature.

The contents of all these works are in themselves a literary curiosity. Both Sanskrit poetry and drama are suffused with a certain amount of poetical sentiment and romance, as are the literatures of other countries. The difference, however, lies in the fact that Sanskrit literature portrays love in a plain, simple and matter of fact manner.

As Venus is the epitome of feminine beauty in Greek literature, the Hindus describe the *padmini,* or the lotus woman, as the perfect representation of the same.

Miniature painting, mid-18th century, Deogarh, Rajasthan. A well-bred townsman, the nayaka, *should dress in rich clothes and sparkling jewels. (Right) The Padmini* nayika, *heroine, has a face as pleasing as the full moon and her bosom is full and hard.*

PADMINI (Lotus Woman)

She in whom the following signs and symptoms appear is called a padmini. *Her face is pleasing as the full moon; her body, well clothed with flesh, is soft as the* shiras, *or mustard flower; her skin is fine, tender and fair as the yellow lotus, never dark colored. Her eyes are bright and beautiful as the orbs of the fawn, well cut, and with reddish corners. Her bosom is hard, full and high; she has a good neck; her nose is straight and lovely, and three folds or wrinkles cross her middle, about the umbilical region. Her yoni, or vagina, resembles the opening lotus bud, and her* kamasalila, *or love seed, is perfumed like the lily that has newly burst. She walks with a swanlike gait, and her voice is low and musical as the notes of the* kokila, *cuckoo bird; she delights in fresh rainments, in fine jewels, and in rich dresses. She eats little, sleeps lightly, and being as respectful and religious as she is clever and courteous, she is ever anxious to worship the gods, and to enjoy the conversation of Brahmins. Such then is the* padmini, *the lotus woman.*

Sanskrit literature then goes on to give detailed descriptions of the *chitrini,* art woman; the *shankini,* conch woman; and the *hastini,* elephant woman. It elaborates their days of enjoyment, their seats of passion, the manner in which they should be wooed and treated during sexual intercourse. It emphasizes the characteristics of men and women from various regions of India. The details are numerous, and the subjects have been dealt with seriously and at very great length.

Introduction

It makes for interesting reading to know how Vatsyayana's *Kama Sutra* was first brought to light and translated into the English language. It happened thus. When *Ananga Ranga* was being translated, frequent references were found to the sage Vatsyayana whose opinions were also quoted. On being asked who this sage was, pundits replied that Vatsyayana was the author of the standard work on love in Sanskrit literature, and no Sanskrit library was complete without his work. But it had become most difficult to obtain the work in its entire state. The copy of the manuscript obtained in Bombay was defective, and so the pundits wrote to Sanskrit libraries in Benares, Calcutta and Jaipur for copies of the same. These were then compared with each other, and with the aid of a commentary called *Jayamangala*, a revised copy of the entire manuscript was prepared, from which the English translation was made.

Aphorisms on Love

Vatsyayana's work contains about one thousand, two hundred and fifty *shlokas*, or verses, and is divided into seven books and thirty-six parts. Hardly anything is known about Vatsyayana himself. His real name was supposedly Mallinaga or Mrillana, Vatsyayana being his

Shiva, god of virility sits majestically on Nandi. One of Hinduism most potent symbols, Shiva's lingam is described as always stiff, always erect. (Right) Parvati, Shiva`s consort seduced him and broke his long trance. She put on enticing clothes, a delightful wreath of gems, lined her crimson eyes with collyrium. Her attractive nipples were covered with lines of painting with cosmetics. Her navel was deep and bright. Her belly was circular and graceful and her thighs put to shame the plantain tree.

family name. At the end of his work, Vatsyayana wrote:

After reading and considering the works of Babhravya and other ancient authors, and thinking over the meaning of the rules given by them, this treatise was composed, according to the precepts of the Holy Writ, for the benefit of the world, by Vatsyayana, while leading the life of a religious student at Benares, and wholly engaged in the contemplation of the Deity. This work is not to be used merely as an instrument for satisfying our desires. A person acquainted with the true principles of this science, who preserves his dharma, *his* artha *and his* kama, *and who has regard for the customs of the people, is sure to obtain mastery over his senses. In short, an intelligent and knowing person,* attending to dharma *and* artha *and also to* kama, *without becoming the slave of his passions, will obtain success in everything that he may do.*

Dharma	Virtue, religious merit
Artha	Worldly wealth
Kama	Love, pleasure, sensual gratification

Though it is impossible to put an exact date on Vatsyayana's life or work, based on certain references in his work, it is presumed that he lived sometime between the first and sixth century A.D. He mentions that Satakarni Satavahana, a king of Kuntala, seized with the passion of love, deprived Malayavati, his wife, of her life by using *kartari,* a highly ardent scissor-like grip. Vatsyayana quotes this to caution lovers of the danger of such practices when under the influence of an all-consuming passion. Since this king of Kuntala is believed to have lived and reigned during the first century A.D., Vatsyayana must have lived after him.

Varahamihira, who is believed to have lived during the sixth century, wrote *Brihatsamhita, the Science of Love.* In the eighteenth chapter he appears to have borrowed largely from Vatsyayana on the subject.

Therefore Vatsyayana must have written his works earlier, though not earlier than the first century A.D., and not later than the sixth century.

There are only two commentaries which have been found on Vatsyayana's work - *Jayamangala* or *Sutrabhashya,* and *Sutravritti.* The date of the *Jayamangala* is fixed between the tenth and thirteenth centuries A.D., because in the description of the sixty-four arts, an example is taken from the *Kavyaprakasha* which was written around the tenth century A.D. Again, the copy of the commentary procured was a transcript of a manuscript which once had a place in the library of a Chalukyan king named Vishaladeva, as is evident from the following sentence at the end of it:

Here ends the part relating to the art of love in the commentary on the Vatsyayana Kama Sutra, *a copy from the library of the king of kings, Vishaladeva, who was a powerful hero, as it were - a second Arjuna, and head jewel of the Chalukya family.*

It is well known that Vishaladeva ruled in Gujarat from A.D. 1244 to 1262, and founded a city called Vishalnagar. The date of the *Jayamangala,* therefore, is taken to be between the tenth and the thirteenth century. It is supposed to be written by one Yashodhara, the name being given to the author by his preceptor Indrapada. He seems to have written it during the time of affliction caused by his separation from a clever and shrewd woman, as he himself says at the end of each chapter. It is presumed that he named his work after his absent mistress, or it may have some connection with the meaning of her name.

This commentary was most useful in explaining the true meaning of Vatsyayana's work, for the commentator appears to have had considerable knowledge of the times of the older author, providing very detailed information in some places.

The same cannot be said of *Sutravritti,* written around A.D. 1789 by Narsing Shastri, a pupil of a Sarveshwar Shastri. The latter was a descendant of Bhaskar, as was this author, for at the conclusion of every part he calls himself Bhaskar Narsing Shastri. He was induced to write this commentary by order of the learned Raja Vrijalala, while he was residing in Benares, but it does not deserve much commendation. In many instances he does not appear to have understood the meaning of Vatsyayana's original work, and has changed the text in many places to fit in with his own explanations.

This book is based on the original Burton and Arbuthnot translation of Vatsyayana's *Kama Sutra,* with additions from other Sanskrit versions.

Kama is a handsome youth who, armed with a bow and a quiver of arrows, tipped with flowers, pursues his quarry of young loves. His thirst for love is shared and dispensed with his wife, Rati Devi. (Left) Shalabhanjika, the celestial nymph – a Kushana sculpture, 1st-2nd century, Govt. Museum, Mathura. Apsaras or celestial nymphs descended from heaven to fulfil preordained purposes.

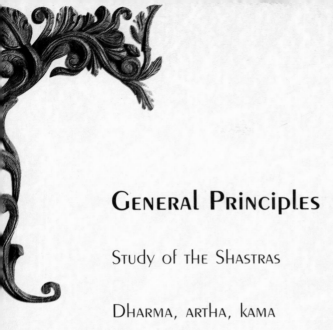

General Principles

Book 1

Study of the shastras

शास्त्रसंग्रह प्रकरण

Shastrasangraha Prakarana

 n the beginning, the Lord of Beings created men and women, and in the form of commandments in one hundred thousand verses, laid down rules for regulating their existence with regard to *dharma, artha* and *kama*. Some of these commandments, such as those which dealt with *dharma,* were written separately by Swayambhu Manu; those that related to *artha* were compiled by Brihaspati; and those that referred to *kama* were expounded by Nandikeshvara, the follower of Mahadeva.

The *Kama Sutra, Aphorisms on Love,* written by Nandikeshvara in one thousand parts, was reproduced in an abbreviated form in five hundred canons, by Shvetaketu, the son of Uddalaka. This work was again similarly reproduced in an abridged

Embellished with exquisite ornaments the nayika curves her body in an alluring pose. (Left) A cave painting from the Vishvantara Jataka, 6th century, Ajanta, Northern Deccan. The nayaka is seen in a pleasure palace.

form, in one hundred and fifty canons, by Babhravya, an inhabitant of Panchala, south of Delhi. The aphorisms were then put together under seven heads:

Sadharana: general principles

Samprayogika: love-play, sexual union

Kanya Samprayuktaka: courtship and marriage

Bharyadhikarika: the wife

Paradarika: seducing the wives of others

Vaishika: the prostitute

Aupanishadika: secret lore, extraneous stimulation and sexual power

The sixth book in this work on *Vaishika*, the prostitute, was separately expounded by Dattaka at the request of the courtesans of Pataliputra, now Patna; similarly Charayana explained the first book, *Sadharana,* general principles.

The remaining subjects were each treated by different authors :

Charayana	-	*Sadharana*	Book I
Suvarnanabha	-	*Samprayogika*	Book II
Gotakamukha	-	*Kanya Samprayuktaka*	Book III
Gonardiya	-	*Bharyadhikarika*	Book IV
Gonikaputra	-	*Paradarika*	Book V
Dattaka	-	*Vaishika*	Book VI
Kuchumara	-	*Aupanishadika*	Book VII

Since the books were written by different authors, it was almost impossible to obtain them. Moreover as each book expounded only a specific subject, it was incomplete as a comprehensive work. The original work of Babhravya was also difficult to master on account of its length. Vatsyayana, therefore, solved this problem by composing his work in a small volume as an abstract of the entire works of all the authors.

DHARMA, ARTHA, KAMA
त्रिवर्गप्रतिपत्ति प्रकरण

Trivargapratipatti Prakarana

 an, the period of whose life is taken to be one hundred years, is advised to practice *dharma, artha* and *kama* at different times and in such a manner that they harmonize together. In his childhood he should acquire learning; in his youth and middle age he should attend to *artha* and *kama,* and in his old age he should perform *dharma,* and seek *moksha,* or release from further transmigration. Or, on account of the uncertainty of life, he may practice them together at times. But it is essential that he should lead the life of a religious student until he finishes his education.

Dharma is obedience to the command of the *Shastras,* the Holy Writ of the Hindus, to commit certain acts. These include the performance of sacrifices, which are not generally carried out

Parvati is the goddess of beauty and exceedingly voluptuous to behold. Her mere presence was sufficient to arouse the uncontrollable desires of Shiva.

because they are offerings to the gods and often produce no visible effect. The *Shastras* forbid certain practices such as eating meat, which are often followed because they are part of material life, with very visible effects.

Dharma should be learned from the *Shruti* and *Vedas,* and from those conversant with it.

Artha implies the acquisition of art, land, gold, cattle, wealth and friends; the protection of what is acquired; and the increase of what is protected. It should be learned from the king's officers, and from merchants who are versed in the practices of commerce.

Kama is the enjoyment of objects by the five senses of hearing, touch, sight, taste and smell, assisted by the mind and the soul. The peculiar contact between the organ of sense and an object, and the consciousness of pleasure which arises from that contact is called *kama*.

Kama is to be learned from the *Kama Sutra - Aphorisms on Love,* and from the experience of citizens.

When all the three, *dharma, artha* and *kama* come together, the former is better than the one which follows it. *Dharma* is better than *artha,* and *artha* is better than *kama.* But *artha* should always first be practiced by the king for the livelihood of men is to be obtained from it only. Again, *kama* being the occupation of *veshyas,* or prostitutes, should be preferred by them to the other two. However there are exceptions to the general rule.

Radha and Krishna in union.(Right) Ravana abducting Rama`s wife Sita in a clear violation of dharma, *for which he had to pay with his life.(Previous Page)Kama makes passionate love to his consort Rati, who signifies lust and sexual delight. Apsaras, or heavenly damsels, the handmaidens of Kama, personify celestial beauty and stand with their hands folded in reverence of this heavenly union.*

Some learned men opine that both dharma *and* artha *can be learnt only from books. But* kama *which is to be found everywhere and practiced even by brute creation does not require any study on the subject.*

This is not so. Sexual intercourse being dependent on man and woman requires the application of proper means by them, and these are to be learned from the *Kama Shastra*. The non-application of proper means which is seen in brute creation is caused by their unrestrained behavior, and sexual intercourse with females during certain seasons only - this intercourse not being preceded by any thought.

The Lokayatikas *say: Religious ordinances should not be observed for they promise a future fruit, and it is doubtful whether they will bear any fruit at all.*

This is not so. The Holy Writ which ordains the practice of *dharma*, does not admit of a doubt.

Sacrifices such as those made for the destruction of enemies or for the fall of rain are seen to bear fruit. The sun, moon, stars, planets and other heavenly bodies appear to work intentionally for the good of the world. The existence of this world is affected by the

observance of the rules respecting the four classes of men and their four stages of life. Vatsyayana is therefore of the opinion that the ordinances of religion must be obeyed.

Everything is in the hands of destiny, which controls gain and loss, success and defeat, pleasure and pain. Thus we see that Bali was raised to the throne of Indra by destiny, and was also put down by the same power, and it is only destiny that can reinstate him.

It is not right to presume that everything is determined by destiny. The acquisition of every object presupposes some exertion on the part of man. It, therefore, follows that even where something is destined to happen, a person who puts in no individual effort will not enjoy happiness.

Those who are inclined to think that artha *is the chief object to be obtained state: Pleasures bring a man distress, and into contact with low persons; they cause him to commit unrighteous deeds, make him impure and uncaring about the future, and encourage carelessness and levity. They cause him to be disbelieved by all, received by none, and despised by everybody, including himself.*

This argument cannot be sustained, for pleasures are as necessary for the existence and well-being of the body as food. Moreover they are the results of *dharma* and *artha*. They should, however, be followed with moderation and caution.

There are some *shlokas*, verses:

Thus a man practicing dharma, artha *and* kama *enjoys happiness both in this world and the world to come. The good perform actions without fear of the result from them in the next world, and without danger to their welfare. Any action which is conducive to the practice of* dharma, artha *and* kama *together, or of any two, or even one of them, should be performed, but an action which encourages the practice of one of them at the expense of the remaining two should not be performed.*

STUDY OF ARTS, SCIENCES

विद्यासमुद्देश प्रकरण

Vidyasamuddesh Prakarana

an should study the *Kama Sutra* and the related arts and sciences, in addition to the study of the arts and sciences contained in *dharma* and *artha*. Young maids should study the *Kama Sutra* and its arts and sciences before marriage and continue to do so after it with the consent of their husbands. Some learned men may disagree and say that women, not being allowed to study any science, should not study the *Kama Sutra*.

But Vatsyayana is of the opinion that this objection does not hold good, for women already know the principles of *Kama Sutra*, and these are derived from the *Kama Shastra*, the science of *kama* itself.

The *Kama Shastra* for Women

A woman, therefore, should learn the *Kama Shastra*, or at least a part of it, by studying its tenets from a confidante. She should spend time alone studying the sixty-four arts that form a part of the *Kama Shastra*. Her teacher should be one of the following: the daughter of a *dhatri*, or nurse, brought up with her and already married; a female friend who can be trusted; her maternal aunt; an old female servant; a *sanyasini*, or female mendicant, who may

have formerly lived in the family; or her own elder sister who can always be trusted.

Complementary Arts

The arts to be studied, as complementary to the *Kama Shastra,* are singing, playing musical instruments and dancing; writing, sketching and painting; cutting leaves into patterns for adorning the forehead; arranging floral decorations on the floor, around the door frame and for rituals; adornment of the household deity with rice, colored powders and blossoms; coloring and painting the nails, palms, and other parts of the body with herbal extracts; staining the teeth, hair and feet; sewing, stitching, mending and dyeing garments; knitting and weaving; camouflaging clothing defects by wearing them ingeniously; stringing necklaces and garlands of flowers in the hair braided in a *shekharaka,* hanging, or *apidaka,* circular fashion.

Draping the bedroom, and other private rooms with colored cloth and flowers appropriate to various seasons and occasions; fashioning of ornaments from animal tusks of ivory, bone, silver and precious materials; extracting perfumes and fragrances from flowers and herbs; learning the culinary arts from experts of different cuisines, making fruit drinks and spirituous extracts with different flavors and colors; imbibing rules of etiquette from older people; and organizing party games with figures of temples, birds, animals and

Radha and Krishna exchange love notes. (Left) Citizens should indulge in arranging parties and festivities appropriate to the days of spring and celebrate in honor of the God of Love. They should sprinkle perfumed water and throw flowers on each other.

symbols animated by colored threads and wound around the fingers; teaching parrots, mynahs and starlings to imitate words.

Intellectual Pastimes

Solving riddles, enigmas, oral puzzles with hidden meaning; reciting verses beginning with the last letter of the verse recited by another person; inventing tongue-twisting phrases, their meanings being distorted when uttered quickly; reading, including chanting and intonation; knowledge of stories, dramas, and legends; completing verses and stories half-composed by others; gaining knowledge of regional languages and their dialects; speaking and

deciphering code words and changing forms of words by interchanging the letters or inserting a letter after every syllable; memorizing literary passages and verses; repeating unfamiliar literary works by reading or hearing them once only; composing poems to include given words; knowledge of dictionaries and vocabularies, and of meters and figures of speech.

Useful Knowledge

Studying architecture, house construction, and repairs; learning gardening and the lore of growing plants and trees, their nourishment and protection from pests; evaluating silver and gold coins and precious gems; extracting metals and mixing them.

Sports

Practicing water sports, striking water to make rhythmic sounds, and diving in various poses; gambling and playing dice; wielding arms; wrestling, boxing and other exercises.

Magic, Sorcery, Aphrodisiacs

Practicing magic and sorcery, and the means

expounded by Kuchumara to augment beauty and sexual power and enhance the effect of medicinal herbs and intoxicants with aphrodisiacal and stimulatory qualities; practicing the ancient art of body massage with hands and feet, and refreshing baths with rare and valuable essential oils; drawing mystical diagrams, intoning spells and charms, binding amulets, discerning between bad and good omens; and covert actions.

Some *shlokas* say:

A veshya, public woman, endowed with a good disposition, beauty and other winning qualities, and also versed in the arts, obtains the name of a ganika, or courtesan of high quality. She receives a seat of honor in an assemblage of men. She is always respected by the king and praised by learned men; her favor is sought by all and she is held in high regard by all. Similarly, the daughter of a king or a minister, also being learned in these arts, can win her husband's favor, even though he may have several other wives besides her. Similarly, if a wife, separated from her husband, falls into distress, she can support herself easily, even in a foreign country, by her knowledge of these arts. Even a brief knowledge of them makes a woman attractive.

A man who is versed in these arts and is loquacious and gallant, very soon gains the hearts of women, even though he may have only been acquainted with them for a short time.

(Top) A Mithuna couple form the decorative sculpture of a temple in Bhubaneshwar. (Bottom) A bronze hair-pin depicts a loving couple. (Left) A love lorn couple in the throes of a passionate embrace.

MAN ABOUT TOWN

नागरकवृत्त प्रकरण

Nagarakavritta Prakarana

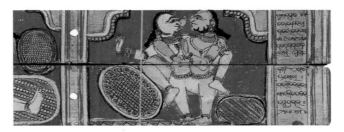

aving thus acquired learning, a man, with the wealth that he may have gained by gift, conquest, purchase, deposit, or inheritance from his ancestors, should become a householder, and live the life of a citizen. He should reside in the vicinity of cultured men in a town, capital city, large village, or place selected for his livelihood. His house should be situated near a source of water, surrounded by a garden with bowers, and divided into different compartments for different purposes. There should be two residential apartments: an outer one and an inner one for privacy.

His Residence

The inner apartment should be occupied by women. The outer one should contain a room, fragrant with rich perfumes; a bed with a soft mattress, low in the middle, and covered with a clean, white sheet; a canopy above and pillows at the head and foot. At the head should be a small niche with an image of the family deity; nearby a stool with jars for perfumed ointments, sweet smelling flowers

(Left) Loving couple, door frame of a Buddhist stupa.

and garlands; pots for collyrium and other fragrant substances, the bark of the common citron tree, and prepared betel nuts and leaves. Near the bed should be a couch; on the ground an engraved brass cuspidor; a lute hanging from a peg made from the tusk of an elephant; a board with paper for sketching and jars containing brushes and paints; a few books, and some garlands of the fragrant yellow amaranth flowers. On the ground near the couch should be a mattress of soft grass, and a *gowtakiya*, barrel-shaped pillow for reclining; a board with dice ought to be placed there too.

Outside this room, there should be bird cages; and separate rooms for study, hobbies, crafts, spinning and weaving. The garden should contain a swing protected by the shade of trees, and bowers of creepers laden with flowers with a raised parterre for sitting.

Daily Lifestyle

After waking up in the morning and performing the necessary ablutions, the householder should wash his teeth, apply a few ointments and perfumes, wear some ornaments, put collyrium on his eyelids and below his eyes, colour his lips with red lac, and eat betel leaves with other ingredients that provide fragrance to his breath.

He should bathe daily and clean his armpits; anoint his body with oil every other day; apply *phenaka,* or herbal soap powder every three days; have his head and face shaved every four days, and the other parts of his body every five or ten days. These practices should be carried out without fail. Meals should be taken in the forenoon, afternoon and at

night, according to Charayana. After breakfast, he should spend some time teaching parrots and other birds to imitate human speech, and enjoy the fighting of cocks, quails and rams. Some time should be devoted to diversions with *pithamardas, vitas* and *vidushakas;* this should be followed by the midday siesta. After this the man about town, donning his clothes and ornaments, should visit his friends in the late afternoon and take part in intelligent amusements. In the evening entertainment should be provided in the form of singing, after which he and his friend should wait in his room, which has been previously decorated and perfumed, for the arrival of the woman who may be attached to him, or he may send a female messenger for her, or go and fetch her himself. On her arrival they should welcome her and entertain her with loving and pleasant conversation. Thus would the diversions of the day be concluded.

In Honor of the Deity

Other diversions or amusements can also be occasionally pursued.

Shiva is mostly symbolized with four arms, with one upper arm holding the damru (a small hand drum) and the other a trident. He wears huge pendant earrings, his hair is matted and a snake coils around it. (Left) Nandi, Lord Shiva's faithful and trustworthy bull companion.

On any auspicious day assigned to the deity, an assembly of citizens should be convened in the temple of Saraswati. There the skill of singers and other recent visitors in the town should be put to the test, and on the following day, they should be given some rewards. Then, depending on the appreciation of their performance by the assembly, they may either be retained or dismissed. The members of the assembly should always act in concert, both in times of distress and prosperity, and it is also their duty to extend hospitality to any strangers who may have come to the assembly. This should also apply to all the other festivals which may be held in honor of different deities, according to the established rules.

Social Activities

When men of the same age, disposition and talents, fond of the same diversions, and with the same degree of education, sit together with society women, or in an assembly of citizens, or at the abode of any one of them, and engage in agreeable discourse, this is called a sitting in company, or a social gathering. The subjects of discourse should comprise the completion of verses half composed by others, and testing each other's knowledge in the various arts. The most beautiful women, who may like the same things as the men, and who may have the power to attract the minds of others, should be paid appropriate homage.

Citizens should organize drinking parties. Society women should first offer liquors such as *madhu, maireya, sura* and *asawa* to the men, along with spicy fruit and vegetable delicacies containing salty, pungent, bitter and sour ingredients, and then eat and drink themselves.

In the morning, after dressing, men should ride out to gardens on horseback, accompanied by society women and followed by servants. They should enjoy the morning amidst pleasurable diversions, such as the fighting of quails, cocks and rams;

(Left) A charming vignette of the nayaka *and* nayika *– miniature painting, mid-19th century, Pahari.*

gambling, and feasting their eyes on dramatics and other performances. Sated, they should return home in the afternoon, taking with them bunches of flowers as mementoes.

During the summer group-bathing can be enjoyed by sporting in the water in wells and tanks, purified with fragrant substances and free of dangerous aquatic creatures.

Celebrating Spring

Citizens should spend *yaksharatri,* the night of light, playing dice and gambling; taking leisurely strolls on moonlit nights, or indulging in outdoor sports; swinging, arranging parties and festivities appropriate to the days of spring and celebrating in honor of the God of Love. They should gather tender leaves and flowers to adorn themselves; sprinkle perfumed water and throw flowers of the *kadamba* tree on each other; mimic with dialogues and sound; and partake in other such sports and amusements which appeal at the time.

Pithamarda: Teaching the Arts

A *pithamarda* is an itinerant, alone in the world, and penniless. Skilled in certain arts, he makes his living amidst assemblies of interested people, and by teaching them to courtesans.

Vita: A Messenger

A *vita* is a married man with a wife, who once enjoyed life's pleasures but has now lost his wealth; he has the qualities of a *nagaraka* even if he is no longer one himself, and is honored in assemblies of citizens and the

A woman learned in the sixty four arts, can win her husband's favor, even though he may have several other wives besides her.

Similarly, a wife who is separated from her husband can support herself easily, by her knowledge of these arts. A man who is versed in these arts and is loquacious and gallant, very soon gains the hearts of women.

abodes of society women. He lives by liaising between *nagarakas* and courtesans.

Vidushaka: A Jester

A *vidushaka,* also called a *vaihasika,* is a jester who provokes laughter; he is trusted by all and is acquainted with some arts. He acts as an adviser, being employed after quarrels to bring about a reconciliation between citizens and society women. This category of advisers also includes wives of Brahmins living on alms.

Some *shlokas* on this subject state:

A citizen discoursing, neither entirely in the Sanskrit language, nor wholly in the dialect of the region, on various topics in society, obtains great respect. The wise should not resort to a society disliked by the public, or one not governed by any rules, and intent on the destruction of others. In fact a learned man living in a society which acts according to the wishes of the people, and which has pleasure as its only object, is highly respected in this world.

Vatsyayana`s nayaka was one who belonged to the affluent cultured class.(Previous page) He organized receptions with music, dancing, singing and instruments. He was always elegantly dressed with jewels and offered drinking and amusements to the guests.

Nayikas and messengers

नायकसहाय-दूतीकर्म प्रकरण

Nayakasahaya-dooti-karma Prakarana

 hen *kama* is practiced by men of the four castes according to the rules of lawful marriage with virgins of their own caste, and according to society's customs, it becomes a means of acquiring lawful progeny and a good name. But the practice of *kama* with women of a higher social level, or with those previously enjoyed by others, even though they are of the same class, is prohibited. The practice of *kama* with women of a lower standing, or with excommunicated women is accepted; but *kama* with prostitutes and women previously enjoyed by others for carnal pleasure only, is neither recommended nor prohibited.

Nayikas: Heroines

Nayikas are of three kinds: *kanya*, maid; *punarbhu*, single woman, either widowed

---

The royal couple in a relaxed mood look fondly at each other. (Left) As the beautiful heroine dresses up in private her maid assists her. In all probability it is the maid who has secretly acted as a messenger and has lead the hero to witness her bare charms.

or deserted by her husband, or who has left her husband; and *veshya*, a prostitute or courtesan.

In Search of a Special *Nayika*

Gonikaputra opines that there is a fourth kind of *nayika*, a woman who is resorted to for some special reason even though she may have been earlier married to another. These special occasions arise when a man thinks:

*This woman is self willed, and has been previously enjoyed by many others besides myself. I may, therefore, safely resort to her as to a prostitute, though she belongs to a higher society than mine, and in so doing, I shall not be violating the ordinances of *dharma*.

*She is a married, unchaste woman and has been enjoyed by others; there is, therefore, no objection to resorting to her.

*Such a woman has gained the heart of her great and powerful husband and exercises mastery over him, who is a friend of my enemy; if, therefore, she unites with me, she will cause her husband to abandon my enemy.

*This woman can turn in my favor the mind of her very powerful husband, who is, at present, angry with me and wishes to do me harm.

*By befriending this woman I shall gain back my friend, or ruin an enemy, or accomplish some other difficult purpose.

> *The man who is ingenious and wise, who is accompanied by a friend, and who knows the intentions of others, as also the proper time and place for doing everything, can win over very easily, even a woman who is very hard to possess.*

(Right) Salabyhanjayikas or tree-supported nymphs are common in Indian sculpture. They are always appropriately dressed with splendid jewelry on their ankles, neck and arms.

*Being united with this woman, I shall do away with her husband to obtain his enormous wealth which I covet.

*The union of this woman with me will bring me much-needed wealth as I am poor and unable to support myself.

*This woman knows all my weak points, yet loves me ardently. If I do not unite with her, she will make my faults public and tarnish my reputation. Or she will accuse me of something gross which I may find hard to refute, and be ruined. Or perhaps she will detach from me her powerful husband who is under her control and unite him with my enemy, or join the latter herself.

*This woman's husband has violated the chastity of my wives. I shall therefore return that injury by seducing his wives.

*I shall take this woman's help to kill an enemy of the king, who has taken shelter with her, and whom I am ordered by the king to destroy.

*The woman I desire is under the control of this other woman. I shall be able to win the former through the latter's influence.

*This woman will bring me a wealthy and beautiful maid who is unapproachable and under the control of another.

*This woman's husband is a bosom friend of my enemy; I shall use her to administer slow poison to him.

For these and other similar reasons the wives of other men may be resorted to, but it must be distinctly understood that this is only allowed for special reasons and not for mere carnal desire.

Other *Nayikas*

Charayana thinks that there is also a fifth kind of *nayika*: a woman who is kept by a minister or who goes to him occasionally; or a widow who accomplishes the purpose of a man with the person to whom she resorts.

Suvarnanabha adds that a woman who lives as an ascetic and a widow may be considered as a sixth kind of *nayika*.

Ghotakamukha says that the daughters of a public woman or a female servant, who are still virgins, comprise a seventh kind of *nayika*.

Gonardiya is of the view that any woman born of a good family, but difficult to approach after she has come of age, is an eighth kind of *nayika*.

But these four latter kinds of *nayikas* do not differ much from the first four kinds, as there is no separate purpose in resorting to them. Therefore, in Vatsyayana's opinion, there are only four kinds of *nayikas*: the maid, the twice-married woman, the public woman, and the woman resorted to for a special purpose.

Women to Be Avoided

Certain women are not to be enjoyed: lunatics; outcasts; those with a loose and viperish tongue; who cannot keep a secret; who have an inordinate sexual urge difficult to satisfy; who are unsightly and unclean, and those who have lost the glow of youth.

Also forbidden are near relations, female friends, masculine women

Radha and Krishna, the eternal lover in a loving embrace with their legs wrapped around each other. As he increases his touches and foreplay she looks lovingly into the eyes of her lord. (Left) An unusual depiction of Shiva in which he embraces numerous adorers who shower their love and affection on him.

and women of holy orders; wives of relations, friends, learned Brahmins and the king.

Babhravya says that any woman who has been enjoyed by five men is a fit and proper person to be enjoyed. But Gonikaputra is of the opinion that even then, the wife of a relation, friend, learned Brahmin or a king should be made an exception.

The Ideal Messenger

A friend is identified as a childhood playmate, one to whom you are bound by an obligation, someone with the same disposition and fond of the same things as you, a fellow student, one familiar with your secrets and faults and whose faults are known to you, a child of your nurse, one with whom you have grown up, or the son of a family friend.

Such a friend should always tell the truth, rise above temptation, be amiable and support your cause, firm of character, free from covetousness, not easily won over by others, and who does not reveal your secrets.

Charayana says that a *nagaraka,* man about town, may form friendships with washermen, barbers, cowherds, florists, druggists, betel-leaf sellers, tavern keepers, goldsmiths, *pithamardas, vitas* and *vidushakas,* and also with his wives.

A person, who is a loyal friend of both the *nagaraka* and the *nayika* is more to be trusted, and is a fit person to act as an intermediary or go-between in matters of amorous love.

A messenger should possess the following qualities: be eloquent, skillful and quick in repartee; bold but well-mannered; knowledgeable and ingenious; sensitive in correctly interpreting facial expressions and gestures; not easily confused or taken aback, and able to face any situation.

This part ends with the *shloka:*

The man who is ingenious and wise, who is accompanied by a friend, and who knows the intentions of others, as also the proper time and place for doing everything, can win over very easily, even a woman who is very hard to possess.

The famous Gyraspur Devi, an entrancingly singular aspect of femininity, sculptured by a master artisan in a style particular to Madhya Pradesh.
(Left) Lord Shiva devised the motion of dance as the most expressive means to convey the symbolism of mudra, *gesture. The Pala dynasty's voluminous and creative sculptural icons portrayed sexual power.*

Love-play and Sexual Union

Book 2

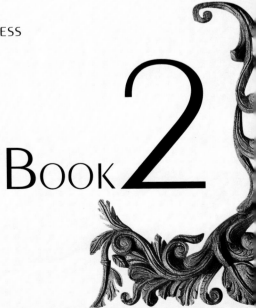

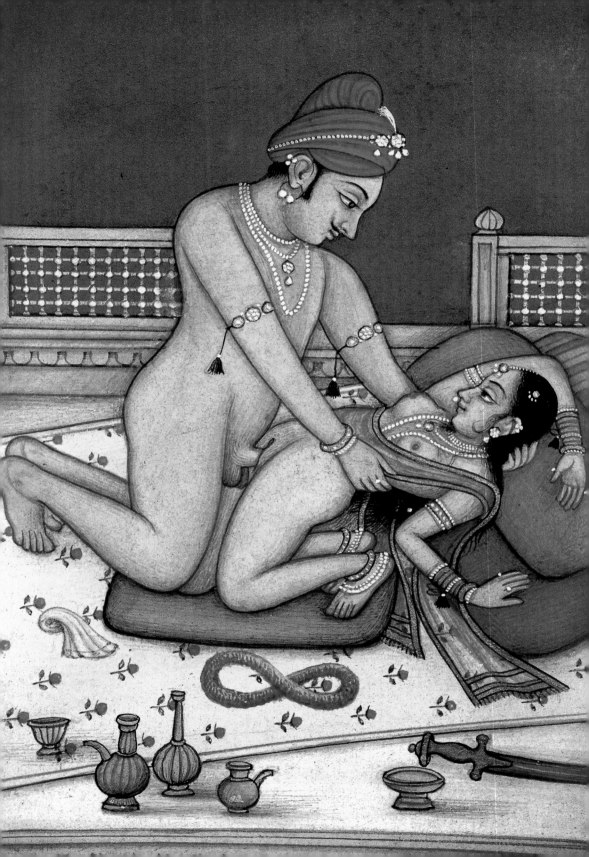

SEXUAL UNION

रतावस्थापन प्रकरण

Ratavasthapana Prakarana

M an is divided into three classes: *shasha*, the hare; *vrisha*, the bull; and *ashwa*, the horse, according to the size of his *lingam*, or phallus.

A woman too, according to the depth of her *yoni*, vagina, is either a *mrigi*, female deer; *vadava,* a mare; or a *hastini*, female elephant.

Equal and Unequal Unions of Dimensions

There are three equal unions between persons of corresponding dimensions and six unequal unions when the dimensions do not

Equal			Unequal	
Male	Female		Male	Female
phallus	vagina		phallus	vagina
Hare	Deer		Hare	Mare
Bull	Mare		Hare	Elephant
Horse	Elephant		Bull	Deer
			Bull	Elephant
			Horse	Deer
			Horse	Mare

(Left) During a high congress, the deer woman should lie down and widen her yoni. Here she lowers her head and raises her middle as she adopts the widely open position.

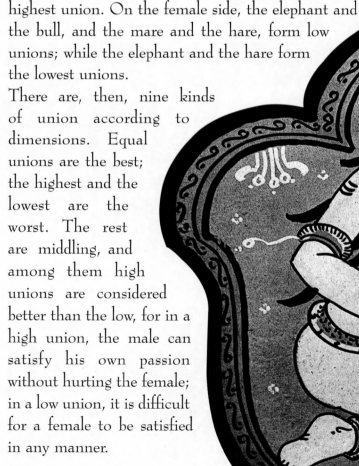

correspond, or nine kinds of unions in all.

In unequal unions, when the male exceeds the female in point of size, his union with a woman immediately next to him in size is called high union and is of two kinds; while his union with a woman most remote from his size is called the higher union and is of one kind only. When the female exceeds the male in point of size, her union with a man immediately next to her in size is called low union and is of two kinds; while her union with a man farthest from her in size is called the lower union and is of one kind only.

In other words, the horse and the mare, and the bull and the deer form the high union; while the horse and the deer form the highest union. On the female side, the elephant and the bull, and the mare and the hare, form low unions; while the elephant and the hare form the lowest unions.

There are, then, nine kinds of union according to dimensions. Equal unions are the best; the highest and the lowest are the worst. The rest are middling, and among them high unions are considered better than the low, for in a high union, the male can satisfy his own passion without hurting the female; in a low union, it is difficult for a female to be satisfied in any manner.

Unions of Passion

There are also nine kinds of union according to the force of passion or carnal desire:

A man of small passion is one whose desire at the time of sexual union is not great, whose semen is scanty, and who cannot bear the warm embraces of the female.

Men of intense passion are full of desire. Yet others who are neither passionate nor indifferent, are those of middling passion.

Similarly, women are supposed to fall into the same three degrees of feeling: small, middling and intense.

Unions of Time

Lastly, based on time, there are three kinds of men and women: the short-timed, the moderate-timed, and the long-timed, and as with the others, there are nine kinds of union.

But in this last category there is a difference of opinion about the female. Auddalika says, "Females do not emit as males do. Males simply remove their desire, while females, from their very consciousness of desire, feel a certain kind of pleasure which gives

This Orissa pata shows Shiva in congress with his consort, Parvati. He holds his lingam in his hand and turns it around in her yoni in an action described as churning. She places her thighs, with her legs doubled on them, on her sides and engages in congress in the position of Indrani.

them satisfaction, but find it impossible to explain what kind of pleasure they feel. This becomes evident because males, when engaged in coition, cease of themselves after emission and are satisfied, but it is not so with females."

However, this opinion is debatable because if a male is long-timed, the female loves him more, but if he is short-timed, she is dissatisfied with him. And this, some say, proves that the female emits too.

On the contrary, if it takes a long time to allay a woman's desire, and during this time she enjoys great pleasure, it is quite natural that she should wish for its continuation. And on this subject there is a *shloka*:

By union with men the lust, desire or passion of women is satisfied, and the pleasure derived from the consciousness of it is called their satisfaction.

But according to the followers of Babhravya, the semen of women

The woman's increased desire is evident as she climbs on to his lover's lap and embraces him. (Right) The nayika *prepares herself in the rising position as she raises both her thighs straight up. The congress takes place in a serene surrounding on the rooftop on a moonlit night. The hero removes his lingam to some distance from the yoni and then forcibly strikes it, described as giving a blow.*

continues to fall from the beginning of the sexual union to its end, and it is right that it should be so, for if they had no semen, there would be no embryo.

There is, however, an opposing view too. At the beginning of coition the passion of the woman is middling and she cannot bear the vigorous thrusts of her lover, but by degrees her passion increases until she ceases to think about her body, and then finally, she wishes to stop further coition.

On this too there is a *shloka*:

The emission of semen, which marks the end of the sexual union, provides the man with the release of his long-sought pleasure; a woman, however, enjoys the union throughout. When they have both shed the semen, then they wish for the discontinuance of sexual intercourse.

Vatsyayana is of the opinion that the semen of the female falls in the same way as that of the male.

Relative Consciousness of Pleasure

Some people wonder why men and women have different reactions when they are beings of the same kind and engaged in bringing about the same results. Vatsyayana believes that this is because their consciousness of pleasure is different. Men are the actors, and women are the persons acted upon, in keeping with their individual natures; otherwise, the actor would sometimes be the person acted upon, and vice versa.

And from this difference in reactions follows the difference in their consciousness of pleasure, for a man thinks, "This woman is united with me", and a woman thinks, "I am united with this man".

It may further be questioned that if the ways of working in men and women are different, why should there not be a difference even in the pleasure they feel?

But this is not true: even though the person acting and the person being acted upon are of different kinds, and there is a difference in their ways of working, there is no reason for any difference in the pleasure they feel, because they both naturally derive pleasure from the act they perform.

There is a *shloka* on this subject:

Men and women, being of the same nature, feel the same kind of pleasure, and therefore a man must first sexually arouse the woman by ardent love play, and then vigorously commence his sex act, so that she reaches the climax earlier or simultaneously with him.

Since there are nine kinds of union with regard to dimensions, force of passion, and duration, their permutations and combinations would produce innumerable kinds of union. Therefore in each particular kind of sexual union, men should use such means as they think suitable for the occasion.

When experiencing sexual union for the first time, the passion of the male is intense and his time is short, but in subsequent unions on the same night, it becomes the reverse. With the female it is the contrary, for during the first time her passion is weak and her time long, but on subsequent occasions on the same night, her passion is intense and her time short.

(Left) The acrobatic stretch of the woman's body allows for a beautiful visual and allows vigorous thrusts and deeper penetration to her lover.

It is a common belief that the man's emission occurs earlier than that of the woman's orgasm.

The following *shloka* states:

According to some ancient sages women with delicate limbs are by nature prone to achieving the climax earlier, as also stout women already excited by kissing, embracing and other outward caressing.

Four Kinds of Love

Men learned in the humanities are of the opinion that love is of four kinds:

Love resulting from the continual performance of an act is called love acquired by constant practice and habit, such as the love of sexual intercourse, hunting, drinking or gambling.

Love which results from ideas to which we are not habituated is called love due to imagination, such as that felt by some men, women, and eunuchs for the auparishtaka, or mouth congress; and that which is felt by all when embraced, kissed, stroked and scratched.

Lovers derive pleasure from the contact of minds along with their bodies. Vatsyayana says sexual games should be played and wagers should be laid to make ground for quarrels, which enhance and intensify passion. (Left) The Rajasthani artist lets his imagination fly in this marvelous piece of art where four loving couples are engaged in passionate love play with their bodies rocking to the motion of a speeding horse.

Love which is mutual and proven to be true, when each looks upon the other as his or her very own, is called love resulting from belief.

Love resulting from the perception of external objects is quite evident and well known to the world, because the pleasure which it affords is superior to the pleasure of other kinds of love, which exists only for its sake.

The foreplay, kissing, embracing and striking which arouse the passions of both the man and the woman to a point where sexual union is a natural culmination, evokes:

* Physical and mental exaltion
* Pleasure from the contact of minds generating love through physical union
* Love which fills the soul and overflows during physical union
* The combination of sexual pleasure and mutual love
* Ecstasy of physical union when the body and spirit conjoin
* Secluded love, enjoyment and peaceful rest
* Lifting of the mind above the mundane

The two lovers walking together in a lonely place, rub their bodies against each other .On this occasion one can also adopt the pressing embrace by pressing the others body forcefully against a support. (Pages 68-69) On a moonlit night the young nayaka takes his sweetheart midstream and attempts to seduce her. His impatience is evident.

THE EMBRACE
अलिंगनविचार प्रकरण

Alinganavichara Prakarana

his part of the *Kama Shastra* deals with sexual union, and is called *Chatushshashti*, or sixty-four. Some authors say it is so titled because it contains sixty-four chapters.

Followers of Babhravya say that this part contains eight subjects: the embrace; kissing; scratching with the nails or fingers; biting; lying down; making various sounds; *purushayitam*, or playing the part of a man; *auparishtaka*, or mouth congress. Each subject is of eight kinds, and since eight multiplied by eight is sixty-four, it is therefore named *Chatushshashti*.

But Vatsyayana affirms that as this part also contains subjects such as striking, crying, the acts of a man during congress, the various kinds of congress and other subjects, the name sixty-four is only accidental.

Kinds of Embraces

Babhravya refers to eight different kinds of embraces:

The embrace which indicates the mutual love of a man and woman

who have come together is of four varieties, and the action is denoted by the word which describes it.

If a man under some pretext goes in front of or alongside a woman and touches her body with his own, he performs the **touching embrace**.

If a woman in a private place bends down as if to pick up something, presses her breasts against a man sitting or standing, and the man takes hold of them, this is called a **piercing embrace**.

These two kinds of embraces take place only between persons who have not, as yet, started speaking freely to each other.

When two lovers walking together slowly, either in the dark, or in a public or a lonely place, rub their bodies against each other, this is referred to as a **rubbing embrace**.

If on this occasion one of them presses the other's body forcibly against a wall or pillar, this is known as a **pressing embrace**.

These two embraces are peculiar to those who know each other's intentions.

Embraces on Meeting

At the time of meeting four kinds of embrace are used:

When a woman clings to a man like a creeper twines around a tree, pulls his head down to hers to kiss him, makes a slight purring sound, embraces him, and looks lovingly at him, this embrace is called **twining of a creeper**.

When a woman places one of her feet on the foot of her lover, and the other on his thigh; passes one of her arms round his back, and the other on his shoulders; makes a slight sound of humming and cooing, and climbs up towards him to get a kiss, this embrace is likened to **climbing a tree**.

These embraces take place when the lover is standing.

When lovers lie on a bed, and embrace each other
so closely that their arms and thighs encircle each
other, and rub against them, this is an embrace
like a mixture of sesamum seed and rice.

If a man and a woman are very much in love and
embrace as if they are entering each other's
bodies, either while the woman is sitting on the
lap of the man, or in front of him, or on a bed,
this is called an embrace like a mixture of milk
and water.

These two kinds of embraces take place at the
time of sexual union.

Embracing Specific Body Parts

Suvarnanabha gives us four more ways of
embracing particular parts of the body:

When one of the two lovers presses one or both
thighs of the other between his or her own forcibly, this is the
embrace of thighs. If a man presses the *jaghana*, middle part of the
woman's body, against his own, and mounts her to practice
scratching with the nail or finger, or biting, or striking, or kissing,
while the hair of the woman remains loose and flowing, this is
referred to as the embrace of the *jaghana*. If a man places his breast
between the nipples of a woman and squeezes them, this is called the
embrace of the breasts. If either of the lovers touches the mouth, eyes
and forehead of the other with his or her own, this is known as the
embrace of the forehead.

Some say that even massaging is a kind of embrace because it
involves touching of bodies. But Vatsyayana thinks that as
massaging is performed at a specific time and for a particular purpose
and has a different character, it cannot be termed an embrace.

*The hero locks his beloved in an embrace of the thighs and attempts to take hold of
her breasts.(Left) The* lataveshtitakam, *creeper embrace. The woman clings to the man,
bending his head down to kiss him. Stone sculpture on wall of Sun Temple, Konarak,
Orissa, 13th century.*

Some *shlokas* further enlighten us on this:
The whole subject of embracing is of such a nature that men who ask questions about it, or who hear about it, or who talk about it, acquire thereby a desire for enjoyment. Even those embraces that are not mentioned in the Kama Shastra *should be practiced at the time of sexual enjoyment, if they are in any way conducive to the increase of love or passion. The rules of the* Shastra *apply as long as the passion of man is middling, but once the wheel of love is set in motion, there is then no* Shastra *and no order.*

The kiss

चुम्बनविकल्प प्रकरण

Chumbanavikalpa Prakarana

ome people opine that there is no fixed time or order between the embrace and the kiss, and the pressing or scratching with nails or fingers. They maintain that these should generally be done before sexual union takes place, while striking and making various sounds should generally take place at the time of the union. Vatsyayana, however, thinks that anything may take place at any time, for love does not care for time or order.
On the occasion of the first congress, kissing, scratching, and so

(Left) The man turns up the face of his nayika *by holding her head and chin and then kisses her, described as a turned kiss. Feeling shy however, she closes her eyes.*

on, should be done moderately, should not be continued for a long time, and should be done alternately. On subsequent occasions the lovers may continue for a long time, and for kindling love, all methods may be used at the same time.

Kissing Spots

The places for kissing are the forehead, eyes, cheeks, throat, bosom, lips, and the interior of the mouth. The people of the Lat country also kiss on the joints of the thighs, the arms and the navel.

Kisses of a Young Girl

For a young girl there are three kinds of kisses:

If a girl only touches the mouth of her lover with her own, but does not initiate any action herself, this is called a nominal kiss.

If a girl, setting aside her bashfulness, wishes to touch the lip pressed onto her mouth and moves her lower lip but not the upper one, this is known as the throbbing kiss.

When a girl touches her lover's lips with her tongue, closes her eyes and places her hands on those of her lover, this is known as the touching kiss.

Other Views on Kisses

If the lips of two lovers are brought into direct contact with each other, this is a straight kiss.

If the heads of two lovers are bent towards each other and they

The nayika *suddenly curves backwards to present her lover with a reverse bent kiss. (Left) Some women of the inner court are amorous and also indulge in oral congress on the yonis of each other. Here they are in the midst of intense desire with their lips sealed in a deep throbbing kiss as their hand explore each others bodies.*

kiss, this described as a bent kiss.

When one of them turns up the other's face by holding the head and chin, and then kisses him/her, it is termed a turned kiss.

In these three kinds of kisses, when one presses the lower lip of the other with great force, this is known as a pressed kiss.

There is also a fifth kind of kiss called the greatly pressed kiss, which is effected by taking hold of the lower lip between two fingers, touching it with the tongue and pressing it with great force with the lip.

Kisses of Passion

A wager may also be laid as to who will get hold of the lips of the other first. If the woman loses, she should pretend to cry, shake her hands, turn away and argue with her lover that "another wager should be laid". If she loses a second time, she should get hold of the man's lower lip and hold it between her teeth so that it does not slip away. Then she should laugh loudly, deride him, dance about, and joke with him, moving her eyebrows and rolling her eyes. These are the wagers and quarrels for kissing, but they may also be applied to pressing or scratching with the nails and fingers, biting and striking. All these, however, are only peculiar to men and women of intense passion.

If a man kisses the upper lip of a woman, and she in return kisses his lower lip, this is referred to as the kiss of the upper lip.

When one of them takes both the lips of the other between his/ her own, it is called a clasping kiss, but a woman only takes this kiss from a man who has no moustache. And during this kiss, if one of them touches the other's teeth, tongue and palate with the tongue, this is called the fighting of the tongue. The pressing of the teeth against the mouth of the other should also be practiced.

Moderate, Pressed, Contracted, Soft

Kissing is of four kinds: moderate, pressed, contracted and soft, according to the part of the body which is kissed, for different kinds of kisses are appropriate for different parts of the body.

If a woman looks at her lover while he is asleep and kisses him to show her desire to unite, this is a kiss that kindles love.

If a woman kisses her lover while he is engaged in business, or quarreling with her, or paying attention to something else, this would be a kiss that turns away.

When a lover coming home late at night kisses his beloved who is asleep on her bed, to show her his desire, this is a kiss that awakens. The woman may pretend to be asleep at the time of her lover's arrival, so that she may get to know his intention and obtain respect from him.

The ivory plaques display a sequence of events elapsed during the lover's secret rendezvous. In the first plaque the woman reaches out to plant a kiss of encouragement to her lover as she finds he is looking elsewhere and his mind is paying attention to something else. Eventually the lovers take alternate sips of wine as their passion takes a feverish pace.

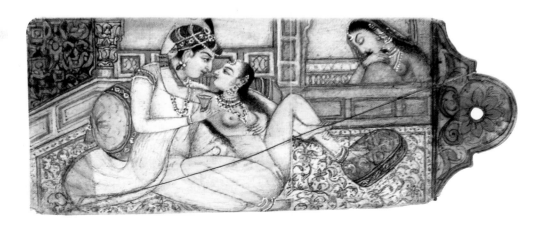

A person who kisses the reflection of the loved one in a mirror, in water, or on the shadow on a wall, gives a kiss showing intention. When a person kisses a child sitting on his lap; or a picture, an image or figure in the presence of the person loved by him, this becomes a transferred kiss.

At night in a theatre, or in an assembly of men of the same caste, when a man comes up to a woman and kisses one finger of her hand if she is standing, or a toe of her foot if she is sitting; or when a woman massaging her lover's body, places her face on his thigh as if she is sleepy, to inflame his passion, and kisses his thigh or great toe, this is called a demonstrative kiss.

There is a *shloka* even on this subject :

Whatever things may be done by one of the lovers to the other, the same should be returned by the other; if the woman kisses him, he should kiss her in return; if she strikes him, he should also strike her in return.

The nayika climbs onto his lap and controls the flow of bodies by encircling her arms around his neck and her legs around his thighs in an embrace like the mixture of milk and water. (Left) The two lovers look lovingly into each other's eyes as their body and spirit conjoin in the ecstasy of their physical union.

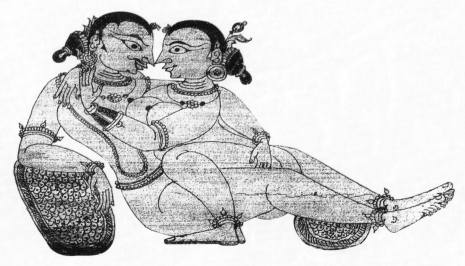

PRESSING AND NAIL MARKS

नखरदनजाति प्रकरण

Nakharadanajati Prakarana

Wh](When) love becomes intense on the following occasions, pressing the other's body with nails or scratching with them is practiced: at the first union, on setting out and return from a journey, when an angry lover is reconciled, when a woman is intoxicated.

However pressing with the nails is not usual except with those who are intensely passionate and full of lust. It is used, together with biting, only by those to whom the practice is agreeable.

Persons with intense passion and wishing to indulge in love-play, should manicure their left-hand finger nails with two or three ridges, as in the blade of a saw. Those with medium passion should make them pointed like the beak of a parrot, and those with less passion should give them the shape of a crescent.

The places that are to be pressed with the nails are the armpit, the throat, the breasts, the *jaghana* or middle parts of the body, and the thighs. But Suvarnanabha feels that when the impetuosity of

(Left) The nayaka contracts his fingers to form a hollow of the palm and fondles the space between the breasts. The relaxed position of the couple indicates the beginning moments of a highly stormy and prolonged session, which is to follow.

passion is excessive, then the places need not be considered.

The qualities of good nails are that they should be bright, well manicured, clean, whole, convex, soft, and glossy in appearance.

Nails are of three kinds according to their size:

Long nails, which give grace to the hands and attract the hearts of women by their appearance, are a quality particular to the people of Bengal.

Short nails, which can be used in various ways and are to be applied only with the object of giving pleasure, are common to the people of the south.

Middling nails, which contain the properties of both the above kinds, are characteristic of the people of Maharashtra.

Pressing with Nails

There are eight kinds of pressing with the nails, according to the forms of the marks which are produced:

When a person presses the chin, breasts, lower lip, or the *jaghana* of another so softly that no scratch or mark is left, but only the hair on the body becomes erect from the touch of the nails, and the nails themselves make a sound, this is called sounding or pressing with the nails. This pressing is used when a lover massages a young girl, scratches her head, and wants to chide or frighten her. The nails are pressed on the back of the neck, and on the breasts to make a deep curve resembling a half-moon.

Here the woman places one of her feet on the feet of her lover and the other on his thigh, passes one arm around his back and other around his shoulders and climbs up to him in order to ordain a kiss, in an embrace that is likened to climbing a tree. (Left) In high intensity of passion pressing or marking with nails is recommended. Special marks on the breasts could resemble the shape of a half-moon, a tiger's nail or a jump of a hare in which five nail marks are made close to one another around the nipple.

The half-moons are impressed opposite each other to form a circle. This mark is generally made on the navel, the small cavities above the buttocks, and on the joints of the thigh.

A mark in the form of a small line, which can be made on any part of the body, is called a line.

When the same line is curved and made on the breast, it is called a tiger's nail.

A mark resembling the imprint of a peacock's foot is made round the nipple by placing the thumb below and the fingers above, and then squeezing gently and firmly. This mark which every woman desires requires great skill and delights her immensely.

When five marks with the nails are made close to one another near the nipple of the breast, they are termed the jump of a hare.

A mark in the form of a leaf of the blue lotus made on the breast or on the hips is called the leaf of a blue lotus.

If a person is going on a journey, and makes a mark of three or four lines impressed close together on the thighs, or on the breasts, this is a token of remembrance.

These are the markings made with nails. Marks of other kinds may

When a woman`s desire remains unsatisfied and her lover is fatigued by copulation, she should lay him down on his back and give him pleasure by enacting his part.
(Left) With her hair loose and flowing the nayika seductively shies away from the amorous advances and embraces of her passionately aroused lover.

also be made with the nails, for pressing or marking with the nails is independent of love, and no one can say with certainty how many different kinds of marks with the nails actually exist. Vatsyayana's explanation for this is that as variety is necessary in love, so also, love is to be produced by means of variety. It is because of this that courtesans, who are well acquainted with the various means of love-sport, become so desirable.

Marks of nails should not be made on another man's wife, but particular kinds of marks may be made on their private parts for remembrance and increase of love.

There are also some *shlokas* on this subject:

The love of a woman who sees the marks of nails on the private parts of her body, even though they are old and almost worn out, becomes again fresh and new. If there be no marks of nails to remind a person of the passages of love, then love is lessened in the same way as when no union takes place for a long time.

Even when a young man casually sees a beautiful maid with the marks of nails on her breasts, he is filled with love and desire for her.

A man who also has the marks of nails and teeth on some parts of his body, influences the mind of a woman, even though it be ever so firm. In short, nothing tends to increase love as much as the effects of marking with the nails and biting.

This enterprising couple matches the rhythm of their moving bodies to the sounds of their lilting love notes. (Left) Lovers embrace as if they are entering each other's bodies. The woman adopts the half-pressed posture by stretching one leg out and contracting the other.

The bite

दशनच्छेद्यविधि प्रकरण

Dashanachhedyavidhi Prakarana

 ll the areas that can be kissed, can be bitten, except the upper lip, the interior of the mouth, and the eyes. Good teeth are equal, pleasingly bright, capable of being colored, of proper proportions, unbroken, and with sharp edges. On the other hand, defective teeth are those that are blunt, rough, soft, large, loosely set and that protrude from the gums.

Healthy Biting

When the teeth are healthy the following kinds of biting can be done:

The hidden bite which is evident only by the excessive redness of the bitten skin.

If the skin is pressed down on both sides, it is called the swollen bite. When a tiny part of the skin is bitten with two teeth only, it is called the point.

When small portions of the skin are bitten with all the teeth, this is referred to as the line of points.

(Left) The couple sculptured on the temple walls at Konarak models the perfect description of the suspended congress. The man leans against a wall, and the woman sits on his hands, which are joined together and under her. She throws her arms around his neck, positions her thighs along his waist, and her feet against the wall and moves herself.

When biting is done by both the teeth and the lips, it is known as the coral and the jewel, the lip - the coral, the teeth - the jewel.

If biting is done with all the teeth, this is called the line of jewels. A bite on the breasts, comprising unequal risings in a circle, which are due to spaces between the teeth, is called the broken cloud.

Bites on the breasts and the shoulders, consisting of broad rows of marks near one another, and with red intervals, are referred to as the biting of a boar. These two last modes of bites are for the intensely passionate.

Female Preferences

In matters of love a man should indulge in such practices as are agreeable to women of different regions. The women of the central regions between the Ganga and Yamuna dislike pressing, nail-scratching and biting. The women of Balhika, Baluchistan, are won over by striking. Maharashtrian women enjoy practicing the sixty-four arts: they utter low, throaty sounds and like to be spoken to in the same way. The women of Pataliputra, or Patna, are like them, but disclose their liking only in secret. The women of Dravida, Tamil Nadu, though rubbed and pressed during intercourse, have a slow fall of semen and are very slow in the act of coition. The women of Vanavasi go through every kind of love-play, cover the marks on their

The man seems to be holding his nayika *to ransom as he plays with her breasts. She holds her hands up in an expression which shows she has given in to his advances without any resistance. (Left) As the* nayika *waits her lover sneaks into her embrace from behind and surprises her by playing with her breasts.*

bodies, and abuse those who utter mean and harsh words. The women of Avanti too hate kissing, marking with nails, and biting, but enjoy various kinds of sexual union. However, the women of Malwa like embracing and kissing, and are won over by striking. The women of Abhira and the Punjab are won over by *auparishtaka,* mouth congress. Aparanta's women are passionate. The women of Lat have impetuous desires and make gasping sounds during intercourse. The women of Stri Rajya and Koshala, Oudh, are similar; their semen falls in large quantities and they are known to take medicine to make it do so. Endowed with tender bodies, Andhra women are fond of enjoyment and voluptuous pleasures. The women of Gauda have tender bodies, and speak sweetly.

A mark resembling the imprint of a peacock's foot is made around the nipple by placing the thumb below the breast and fingers above, and then squeezing it gently but firmly. This mark is desired by every woman and delights her immensely. (Left) When engaged in congress, if the woman turns her middle part around like a wheel, they perform the top, which provides for highly voluptuous pleasure. The posture requires practice, adroitness and a highly flexible torso.

Of all the actions of embracing, kissing, and pressing, those which increase passion should be done first, and those which are only for amusement or variety should be done afterwards.

The *shlokas* on this subject state:

When a man bites a woman forcibly, she should angrily do the same to him with double force. Thus a point should be returned with a line of points, and a line of points with a broken cloud. If the woman is excessively chafed, she should begin a love quarrel with the man at once. At such a time she should take hold of her lover by the hair, bend his head down, and kiss his lower lip, and then, being intoxicated with love, she should shut her eyes and bite him in various places. Even by day, and in a place of public resort, when her lover shows her any mark that she may have inflicted on his body, she should smile at the sight of it, and turning her face as if she is going to chide him, she should show him with an angry look the marks on her own body that have been made by him. Thus if men and women act according to each other's liking, their love for each other will not lessen even in one hundred years.

The hero closely envelops his lover into his arms as he craves to kiss her. (Pages 96-97) The woman adopts the high-pressure posture to compensate for the sexual capacities of her huge partner. This kind of unequal union where a bull man takes a hind woman requires her to fold both legs and open her thighs. The man, presses his chest against her retracted legs, crushes her chest and possesses her.

Sexual vigor

and intensity

संवेशनप्रकार प्रकरण

Samveshanaprakara Prakarana

uring a high congress, the *mrigi*, deer woman, should lie down and widen her *yoni*, while in a low congress, the *hastini*, elephant woman, should contract hers. But in an equal congress, a woman should resort to a natural position. This also applies to the *vadava*, mare woman. In a low congress, the woman is advised to make use of an artificial *lingam* so that her desires are satisfied quickly.

Love Positions

The deer woman can lie down in three ways:

If she lowers her head and raises her middle parts, she adopts the widely opened position. The man should apply an unguent to make the entrance easy.

If she raises her thighs and keeps them wide apart and engages in congress, she is in the yawning position.

When she places her thighs, with her legs doubled on them, on her sides, and engages in congress, she takes the position of Indrani;

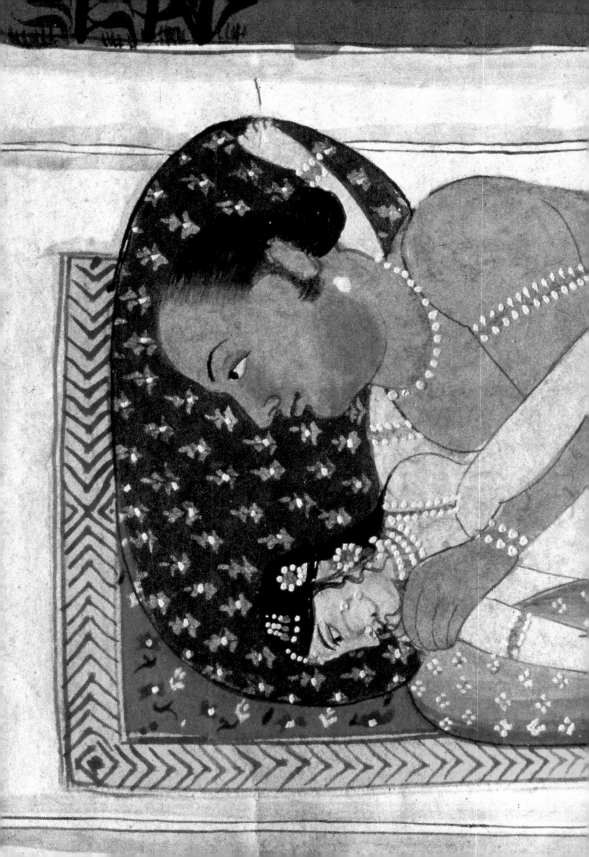

this position and can be learned only through practice.

If the legs of the male and the female are stretched straight out over each other, they adopt the clasping position. This position is of two kinds, the side position and the supine position. In the side position, the male lies on his left side and makes the woman lie on her right side; this should be done with all kinds of women.

The clasping position is used in low congress, together with the pressing position, the twining position, and the mare's position.

After copulation has begun in the clasping position, if the woman presses her lover with her thighs, she adopts the pressing position. When the woman places one of her thighs across the thigh of her lover, this position is called the twining position.

When a woman forcibly holds in her *yoni* the *lingam* after it is in, she takes on the mare's position. This needs practice and is common among the women of Andhra.

These are the different ways of lying down, as mentioned by Babhravya. Suvarnanabha, however, adds the following:

When the woman raises both her thighs straight up, she is said to be in the rising position. If she raises both her legs and places them on her lover's shoulders, she is in the yawning position.

When the legs are contracted and held thus by the lover before his bosom, this is referred to as the pressed position.

(Right) Once the wheel of love starts turning, passionate actions and amorous movements arise on the spur of the moment and are as irregular as dreams.

If only one of her legs is stretched out, she is in the half-pressed position.

When the woman places one of her legs on her lover's shoulder, and stretches the other out, then switches positions, and continues to do so alternately, this is known as the splitting of a bamboo.

If she places one leg around the man's head, and stretches out the other, she is fixing a nail. This is learned by practice only.

When both the legs of the woman are contracted, and placed on her stomach, she is said to be in the crab's position.

If the thighs are raised and placed one upon the other, this is termed the packed position.

When her shanks are upon each other, she takes the lotus position.

During congress, if a man turns around and enjoys the woman again, while she continues to embrace him round the back, they are said to be in the turning position; this too needs practice. Suvarnanabha advises the practice of different ways of lying down, sitting and standing in water, because it is easy to do so. But Vatsyayana is states that this is forbidden by religious law.

If a man and a woman support themselves on each other's bodies near a wall and engage in congress while standing, this is a supported congress.

When a man leans against a wall, and the woman sits on his hands which are joined together and held under her, and throws her arms round his neck, positions her thighs along his waist, and her feet against the wall, and moves herself, this is described as a suspended congress.

When a woman bends on her hands and feet like a quadruped, and her lover mounts her like a bull, this is the congress of a cow.

In the same way can be carried on the congress of a dog, goat, cat, deer; the jump of a tiger; the pressing of an elephant; the rubbing of a boar, and the mounting of an ass or a horse. In all these, the characteristics of these different animals should be manifested by acting like them.

When a man enjoys two women at the same time, both of whom love him equally, this is known as a united congress.

When a man enjoys many women together, this is referred to as the congress of a herd of cows.

The congress of an elephant with many female elephants which is said to take place only in the water, the congress of a collection of goats, or of deer, take place in imitation of these animals.

In Gramanari, Naga Pahari Desh, the northern hill region, and in Stri Rajya, kingdom of women, many young men enjoy a woman who may be married to one of them, either one after the other or at the same time. Thus one of them holds her, another enjoys her, a third uses her mouth, a fourth holds her middle part, and in this way they enjoy several parts of her alternately. This can also be done when several men are in the company of a courtesan, when many courtesans are sporting with one man, or by the women of the king's harem when they providentially get hold of a man.

The people in the south also practice congress in the anus.

These are the various kinds of congress. Two *shlokas* state:

An ingenious person should multiply the kinds of congress, performing them after the fashion of the different kinds of beasts and of birds.

These different kinds of congress, performed according to their prevalence and practice, and the liking of each individual, generate love, friendship and respect in the hearts of women.

(Left) The handsome prince enters his harem and enjoys the congress of a herd of cows with his six selected beauties, two of whom he supports on his thighs, while the others await their turn.

Striking and spontaneous sounds

प्रहणनसीत्कार प्रकरण

Prahananasitkara Prakarana

exual intercourse with its contrarieties can be compared to a combat. The special places for striking with passion on the body are: the shoulders, head between the breasts, back, *jaghana*, and the sides.

Striking is of four kinds: with the back of the hand, the fingers contracted to form a hollow of the palm, the fist, the open palm.

Since it causes pain, striking gives rise to *sitkrita*, hissing, and other sounds akin to crooning in ecstasy: *hinkara*, nasal; *stanita*, purring; *koojita*, cooing; *rudita*, whimpering; *sutkrita*, gasping; *dutkrita*, moaning; and *futkrita*, the sound of a serpent.

There are also words such as Amba, O mother, O god, and those that express satisfaction, pain or praise, to which may be added

(Left) The two men enjoy fondling and pressing the breasts of their beloved nayikas as a curious attendant, obviously excited himself, looks on.

sounds of the dove, cuckoo, pigeon, parrot, bee, sparrow.

Modes of Striking

Fist should be given on the woman's back, while she sits on the man's lap; in turn, she should give blows, abusing the man as if annoyed, while cooing and whimpering. When engaged in sexual union, the couple should fondle the space between the breasts and the breasts slowly at first, and then increasingly so. At this time, *hinkara,* the nasal sound, and other sounds may be made alternately, or at random.

When the man strikes the woman on the head, with the fingers of his hand contracted, he performs *prasritaka.* The woman should coo, and at the end of congress, sigh, whimper and weep.

An innovative cry is *phatakum* - imitating a bamboo being split, while the sound *phat* is like something falling in water. Whenever love-play commences, the woman may reply with a hissing sound. During heightened excitement she should utter words expressive of satisfaction, sigh, whimper and gurgle. Towards the climax, her breasts, *jaghana* and sides should be pressed with open palms , using such pressure as the moment dictates.

There are two *shlokas* on this subject:

The characteristics of manhood are said to consist of roughness and

---

The woman displays tremendous body flexibility, as she stands on her head in an inverted V while also holding the lingams of her master's two attendants.

impetuosity; while weakness, tenderness, sensibility, and an inclination to turn away from unpleasant things are the distinguishing signs of womanhood.

The excitement of passion, and peculiarities of habit may sometimes cause persons to act contrary to their nature, but this does not last long, and in the end the natural state is resumed.

Personal Peculiarities

Using the hands to form a wedge between the bosom, or a scissor-like grip on the head; piercing with the fingers on the cheeks; and pincer-like motions on the breasts and sides, may also be combined with the other four modes of striking. But these four hand formations are unusual and particular to the people of the south. The marks are seen on their women's bodies. Vatsyayana opines that these practices can be painful, barbarous, base, and not always worthy of imitation. Similarly, a personal vice should not be adopted and even if it exists, excess should be controlled.

Some *shlokas* on the subject state:

About these things there cannot be either enumeration or any definite rule. Copulation having once commenced, passion alone gives birth to all the acts of the parties.

Such passionate actions and amorous gesticulations or movements, which arise on the spur of the moment, and during sexual intercourse, cannot be defined, and are as irregular as dreams.

A horse having once attained the fifth degree of motion, goes on with blind speed, regardless of pits, ditches and posts in his way; in the same manner a loving pair becomes blind with passion in the heat of bodily union and goes on with great impetuosity, paying not the least regard to excess.

For this reason one who is well acquainted with the science of love, and knows his own strength, as also the tenderness, impetuosity and strength of the woman, should act accordingly.

The various modes of enjoyment are not for all times or for all persons, and should only be used at the proper time, and in the appropriate places.

DONNING THE MALE ROLE

पुरुषायित प्रकरण

Purushayita Prakarana

 hen a woman's desire remains unsatisfied and her lover is fatigued by copulation, she should with his permission, lay him down on his back, and give him pleasure by enacting his part. She may also do this to satisfy the curiosity of her lover, or because of her own desire for novelty.

There are two ways of doing this. The first is when during congress, she turns round and gets on top of her lover while continuing the congress, without obstructing its pleasure. The other is when she acts the man's part from the start. With flowers in her hair which hangs loose, smiles interspersed with hard breathing, she should press her lover's bosom with her breasts, and lowering her head frequently, act as he did earlier, returning his blows and chaffing him, saying: "I was laid down by you, and fatigued with hard congress; I shall now lay you down in return". She should then again manifest her own bashfulness, her fatigue, and her desire of stopping the congress.

(Left) When a girl takes control over the situation and lies on top of the man and makes love to him it is known as inverted sexuality.

Pleasing the Woman

While the woman is lying on his bed, absorbed in conversation, the man should loosen her undergarments, and when she begins to protest, he should overwhelm her with kisses. Then when his *lingam* is erect, he should touch her with his hands in various places, and gently manipulate various parts of her body. If the girl is bashful and it is their first union, he should place his hands between her thighs, which she will probably keep close together. If she is a young girl, he should first put his hands on her breasts, which she would probably cover with her own hands, and under her armpits and on her neck. If however she is seasoned, he should do whatever is agreeable to him or to her and fitting. After this he should hold her hair and chin in his fingers to kiss her. A young girl will become bashful and close her eyes. But he should deduce from her actions what would be pleasing to her.

Here Suvarnanabha says that while a man is doing what he likes best during intercourse, he should also rub her *yoni* with his *lingam*, with which she will surely roll her eyes to mutely express her delight. Her passion will then be satisfied. This is his reading of women, as they usually maintain silence on such matters.

A woman's enjoyment and satisfaction are obvious when her body relaxes: closing her eyes, she shows an increased willingness to unite the two organs closely together. The signs of her need for

These round ganjifas, playing cards from Orissa portray two young lovers in the midst of their passionate foreplay. (Left) An unusual but interesting variation of the woman on top posture where the nayika raises both legs straight up in the air. The hero supports her thighs by encircling his arms around them.

more enjoyment and failing to be satisfied are: she shakes herself, does not let the man get up, feels dejected, bites the man, kicks him, and continues to go on moving after the man has finished. In such cases, the man should rub her *yoni* with his hand and fingers before engaging in congress, until it is moistened and quivering, and then put his *lingam* inside her.

The *Lingam* and the *Yoni*

After inserting his *lingam* into the *yoni*, the man performs different actions, some of which are described:

If the organs are brought together properly and directly, this is called moving the organ forward.

If the *lingam* is held in the hand and turned around in the *yoni*, it is called churning.

If the *yoni* is lowered, and the upper part of it struck with the *lingam*, this is piercing.

When the same thing is done on the lower part of the *yoni*, it is known as rubbing.

When the *yoni* is pressed by the *lingam* for a long time, it is called pressing.

When the *lingam* is removed to some distance from the *yoni*, and then forcibly strikes it, this is known as giving a blow.

If only one part of the *yoni* is rubbed with the *lingam*, it is described as the blow of a boar.

If both sides of the *yoni* are rubbed in this way, it is known as the blow of a bull.

When the *lingam* is in the *yoni*, and moved up and down frequently without being taken out, this is referred to as the sporting of a sparrow and takes place at the end of the congress.

When a woman acts the part of a man, she can do the following in addition to the nine given above:

When she draws the *lingam* into her *yoni*, and presses it inside her for a long time, this is described as a pair of tongs.

While engaged in congress, when the woman turns around like a

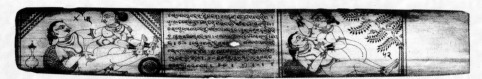

wheel, this is known as the top. This is learnt only by practice.

If the man lifts the middle part of his body, and the woman turns her middle part around, they perform a swing.

If the woman is tired, she should put her forehead on that of her lover, without disturbing the union of the organs; after she feels rested, the man should turn and begin the congress again.

Some *shlokas* on the subject state:

Though a woman is reserved, and keeps her feelings concealed, yet when she gets on the top of a man, she shows all her love and desire.

A man should gather from the actions of a woman of what disposition she is, and in what way she likes to be enjoyed.

A woman during her monthly courses, a woman who has been lately confined, and a fat woman should not be allowed to act the part of a man.

Sometimes carried away by passion a woman puts aside her natural temperament and acts the part of the man by slapping and beating him or play fighting with him. She, at the height of the excitation becomes hard and fearless and dominates the boy, who responds by whining and groaning.(Following page) Those with feminine appearance show it by their dress, speech, laughter, behavior, gentleness and modesty. They arrange their hair in female fashion and imitate their way of talking. They earn their living by performing the act that takes place between the thighs and in the mouth.

ORAL CONGRESS

औपरिष्टक प्रकरण

Auparishtaka Prakarana

here are two kinds of *tritia-prakriti,* or third sex: those that appear as males; and those that are disguised as females, but are males, and by some quirk of nature are feminine in their outlook, exhibiting effeminate characteristics in their dress, speech, gestures, tenderness, timidity, softness and bashfulness.

The acts usually carried out on the *jaghana* of women, are done in the mouth: this is called *auparishtaka,* or mouth congress. These persons derive an imaginary pleasure and their livelihood from this kind of oral sex, and lead the life of masseurs.

The Third Sex

Many males keep their desires secret, but when they wish to indulge their secret urges, they don the life of masseurs. Under this pretense, a male so inclined embraces and draws towards himself the thighs of the man he is massaging, and after this he touches his joints, thighs, *jaghana* and sex organs. Then, if he finds the

(Left) This is highly curvaceous variation of kakila, *the crow where the lovers lie down in an inverted position and are presented with the clear stimulating view of each other's organs and posteriors while carrying on oral sex.*

lingam of the man erect, he presses it with his hands and chaffs him for getting into that state. If after this, and knowing his intention, even though the man does not encourage him to proceed, the masseur does so and begins oral sex. If he is ordered to do so by the man, he first argues with him, and only consents with some persuasion.

The following eight actions are carried out one after the other on the *lingam*: *nimitam,* nominal touch by the lips; *parshwatodashtam,* biting the sides; *bahihsandamsha,* pressing outside; *antahsandamsha,* pressing inside; *chumbitakam,* kissing; *parimrishtakam,* licking; *amrachushitakam,* sucking a mango; *sangara,* swallowing.

At the end of each of these, the passive partner pauses, kindling the other's desire for more excitement and then responds to his entreaties because of the passionate, aroused state he is in then.

The various actions on the *lingam* are described as follows:

Holding the man's *lingam* with his hand, and placing it between his lips, he moves his mouth over the *lingam*.

Covering the end of the *lingam* with his fingers collected together, he presses the sides of it with his lips, also using his teeth.

If the man asks the masseur to proceed, the latter presses the end of the *lingam* with closed lips, kissing it as if drawing it out.

When asked to continue, he draws the *lingam* further into his mouth, presses it with his lips and then takes it out.

Taking the *lingam* in his hand, he fondles and plays with it, then kisses the erect *lingam* as if it were the lower lip.

After kissing it, he touches it with his tongue everywhere, and passes the tongue over the end of the *lingam*.

He then puts half of it into his mouth, kissing and sucking it.

Finally, with the man's consent, he puts the whole *lingam* into his mouth, pressing it to the very end, as if going to swallow it.

(Right) When a man enjoys many women together, all of whom like each other and have the same tastes it is referred to as the congress of a herd of cows. This kind of group sex play falls under special practices.

Striking, scratching, and so on can also be practiced during this kind of oral sex.

Auparishtaka is also practiced by *kulata,* unchaste, and *svairini,* wanton women, female attendants and maid servants, and unmarried women who earn their livelihood by massaging.

Whither Oral Sex?

The *acharyas* felt that *auparishtaka* should not be tried, because it was opposed to the orders of the Holy Writ, and the man suffered by bringing his *lingam* into contact with the mouths of youths and women. But Vatsyayana says that the Holy Writ does not affect those who resort to prostitutes, male and female; the law prohibits the practice of *auparishtaka* with married women only. Moreover injuries to the male can easily be remedied.

He adds that in everything connected with love, a person should act according to custom and inclination. He also recognizes a difference of opinion among knowledgeable men on this subject and admits to an alternative interpretation of the texts.

Some *shlokas* on this topic state:

The male servants of some men carry on the practice of mouth congress with their masters. It is also practiced by close friends among themselves.

When some women of the inner court are amorous, they indulge in oral congress on the yonis *of each other, and some men indulge in the same thing with women. The manner of kissing the* yoni *may be similar to that of kissing the mouth.*

When the woman performs oral congress with a man, it is described as sadharana, *ordinary; when she performs it with her maid, it is known as* asadharana, *extraordinary.*

Young masseurs, usually wearing ear ornaments, do allow their friends as well as some other men to engage with them in oral congress.

Sometimes young actors or dandies allow undersexed or older men to have oral sex with them.

This practice is also followed by young men who know each other well.

Sometimes men who are effeminate indulge in oral sex with each other simultaneously, by lying alongside one another inversely.

When a man and woman lie down in an inverted position, with the head of the one towards the feet of the other, and carry on oral sex, this is called kakila; this term is also applicable to oral congress between two males or two girls or women.

Summing up this uncommon way of enjoyment, the *shlokas* state:

For the sake of such things courtesans abandon men possessed of good qualities, liberal and clever, and become attached to low persons, such as slaves and elephant drivers.

Auparishtaka, *mouth congress*, should be avoided by a learned Brahmin, by a minister who looks after matters of state, or by a man of good reputation, because though the practice is allowed by the Shastras, there is no reason why it should be carried on, and indeed, should only be practiced in particular cases.

This variation of the kakila posture requires great flexibility in the woman's body as her lover spreads her legs wide in an attempt to reach deeper.

There are some men, places and times, with respect to which these activities can be resorted to. A man should therefore pay regard to the place, time, and practice which is to be carried out, as also to whether it is agreeable to his nature and to himself; then only should he decide to indulge in or refrain from these practices.

Some amorous lonely maidens indulge in congress on the yonis of one another. Here one experienced lover skillfully manipulates the others yoni with the help of a well-oiled dildo. (Left) The man widens his lady's already stretched out leg and supports it to allow him a clear unobstructed passage and deeper penetration. This is described as the wild boar's thrust where only one side of the yoni is rubbed with the lingam.

Beginning and end of congress

रतारम्भावसानिक प्रकरण

Ratarambhavasanika Prakarana

I n the pleasure-room, decorated with flowers, and fragrant with perfumes, attended by his friends and servants, the man should receive the woman, who will come bathed and dressed.

Love-play

Inviting a woman to partake of refreshment and drink freely, the man should seat her on his left. Then holding her hair, and touching the end of her garment, he should gently embrace her with his right arm. They can converse lightly on various subjects, including those considered coarse or unmentionable in society. They may enjoy singing with gestures, playing musical instruments, talk about the arts, and persuade each other to drink.

At last when the woman is overcome with love and desire, the man should dismiss his friends, giving them flowers, perfumes, and betel

---

(Left) This miniature painting, early 19th century, Sirohi, Rajasthan, is part of a series which instructs in the erotica.

leaves. Such is the beginning of love-play.

After Congress

After enjoying each other, the lovers should modestly, without looking at each other, go separately for a wash. Then, sitting in their places, they should chew betel leaves, and the man should apply pure sandalwood paste or another unguent to the woman's body. Embracing her fondly, and with agreeable words, he should encourage her to drink from a cup held in his hand. They can partake of sweetmeats; drink soup and fresh juice, including that of the mango; eat meat, the extract of the juice of the citron tree mixed with sugar, or anything else that is sweet, soft and pure.

They may also sit on the terrace of the mansion and enjoy the moonlight, while carrying on an agreeable conversation. During this time, while the woman lies in his lap with her face towards the moon, the lover should show her the different planets, the morning star, the polar star, and *Saptarishis,* the Great Bear.

The Sixty-four Arts

When a man and a woman, in love with each other for some time, come together with great difficulty; or when one returns from a journey, or they reconcile after a quarrel, they unite in loving congress as per their liking and for as long as they choose.

When two persons unite while their love for each other is still in its infancy, this is known as the congress of induced love.

When a man carries on congress by exciting his beloved through the sixty-four ways, including kissing and embracing; or when a man and a woman unite, though they are actually attached to other partners, this is called temporary love. At this time all the methods mentioned in the *Kama Shastra* should be employed.

(Right) The warrior hero returns from the battlefield to a grand reception by his lover.

Throughout a sexual union, if a man imagines that he is enjoying another woman whom he loves, this is actually transferred love.

Congress between a man and a water carrier, or a servant of a caste lower than his own, lasting only till the physical desire is satisfied, is likened to impotent love. Here external touches, kisses and manipulations are kept to the minimum.

Love between a courtesan and a rustic, and between a *nagarika* and a woman of a village or distant country, is deceitful congress.

The sexual union of two persons who are attached to one another, and which is achieved according to their own liking, is spontaneous congress, and is most enjoyable.

A woman who is very much in love with a man cannot bear to hear her rival's name mentioned, to have any conversation about her, or be addressed by her name by mistake. If this happens, a great quarrel arises; the woman cries, becomes angry, tosses her hair, strikes her lover, falls from her bed or seat, casts aside her garlands and ornaments, and throws herself on the ground.

The lover should reconcile her with soothing words, pick her up gently and place her on her bed. Not replying to his questions, and with increased anger, she should pull down his head by pulling his hair, and having kicked him several times on his arms, head, bosom or back, should then rush out of the room.

Dattaka adds that she should then sit angrily outside the door and shed tears. After some time, when she thinks that the conciliatory words and actions of her lover are satisfactory, she should embrace him, reproach him with harsh words, while simultaneously showing him a loving desire for reunion.

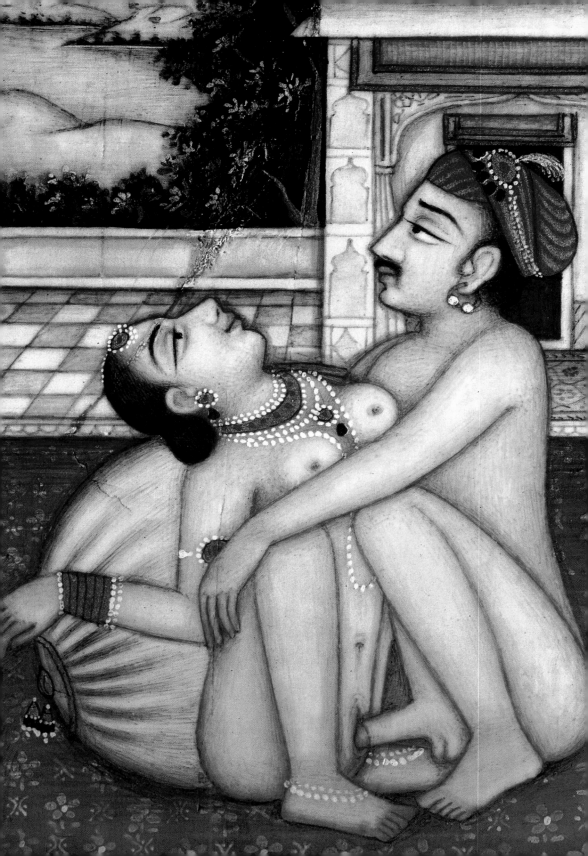

When the woman is in her own house, and has quarreled with her lover, she should go to him and show how angry she is, and leave him. Only later when the citizen sends the *vita*, the *vidushaka* or the *pithamarda* to pacify her, should she accompany them to his house, and spend the night with her lover.

Some *shlokas* proffer:

A man, employing the sixty-four arts mentioned by Babhravya, obtains his object, and enjoys congress with women of the first quality. Though he may speak well on other subjects, if he does not know the sixty-four divisions, no great respect will be paid to him.

A man, devoid of other knowledge, but well acquainted with the sixty-four arts, becomes a nayaka, *leader, in any society of men and women. What man will not respect the sixty-four arts, considering that they are respected by intellectuals, by the cunning, and by courtesans? Since the sixty-four arts command respect, increase the charm in a relationship, and add to the talent of women, they are regarded by the* acharyas *as dear to women. A man skilled in the sixty-four arts is looked upon with love by his own wife, by the wives of others, and by courtesans.*

A woman who is very much in love cannot bear to hear her rival's name. If this happens a quarrel arises. She becomes angry, cries, tosses her hair and kicks and strikes her lover. (Left) The couple makes ardent love in the sitting position. The woman sighs with contentment and draws support from a thick bolster as her hero draws pleasurable moans from her.

Courtship and Marriage

Book 3

Betrothal and marriage

वरणसंविधान प्रकरण

Varanasamvidhana Prakarana

 hen a girl of the same caste and who is a virgin, is married in accordance with the Holy Writ, the results of such a union are: the acquisition of *dharma* and *artha,* offspring, affinity, increase of friends, and untarnished love. A man should, therefore, fix his affections upon a girl of a highly respectable family, whose parents are alive, and who is at least three years younger than him. She should be rich and well connected, with many relations and friends. She should also be beautiful; of a good disposition; with lucky marks on her body; and with good hair, nails, teeth, ears, eyes, and breasts, and not troubled with a sickly body. The man should, of course, also possess these qualities. But in all events, says Ghotakamukha, it would be reproachable to court a girl who has been already joined with another.

Arranging a Marriage

To arrange a marriage with a *kanya,* virgin maid, the man's parents, relations and common friends whose assistance may be desired,

(Left) Dressed in all her finery Goddess Parvati seats herself on her husband Shiva's lap as he embraces her and plays with her left nipple.

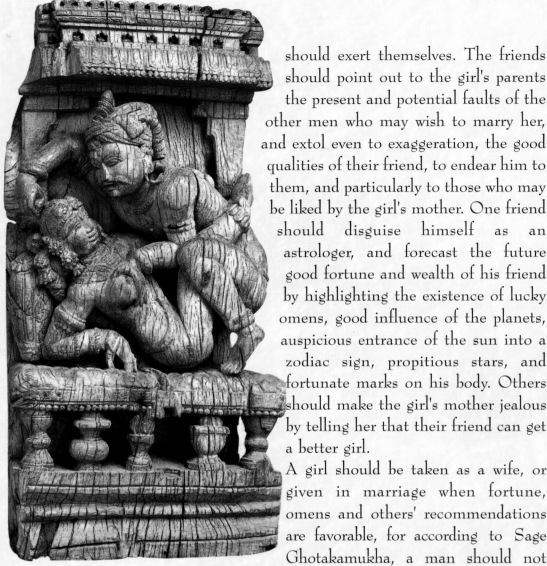

should exert themselves. The friends should point out to the girl's parents the present and potential faults of the other men who may wish to marry her, and extol even to exaggeration, the good qualities of their friend, to endear him to them, and particularly to those who may be liked by the girl's mother. One friend should disguise himself as an astrologer, and forecast the future good fortune and wealth of his friend by highlighting the existence of lucky omens, good influence of the planets, auspicious entrance of the sun into a zodiac sign, propitious stars, and fortunate marks on his body. Others should make the girl's mother jealous by telling her that their friend can get a better girl.

A girl should be taken as a wife, or given in marriage when fortune, omens and others' recommendations are favorable, for according to Sage Ghotakamukha, a man should not marry whenever he likes. A girl who is asleep, crying, out of the house when sought in marriage, or betrothed to another, should not be married.

The following kind of girl should be avoided: one with an ill-sounding name; concealed in the house due to bodily defects;

Being of a tender nature, women desire gentle beginnings. If they are forcibly approached by men with whom they are slightly acquainted, they can become fearful of a sexual relationship. So a man must inspire confidence in her. Only when she has finally overcome her bashfulness, he should begin to enjoy her in such a way as to delight her. (Right) The lonesome nayika plays the veena and attracts a pair of fawns.

engaged to another; with white spots on the body; manly and heavily built; with drooping shoulders or a hunchback; with crooked thighs, receding hair, or abnormally expansive hips; who is in mourning; already enjoyed by another; unchaste; dumb; *mitra,* looked upon as a friend; *svanuja,* regarded like a younger sister, and *varshakari,* with profusely perspiring hands and feet.

Similarly, a girl whose name is that of a tree, a river, one of the twenty-seven stars, or whose name ends in the letters R or I, is considered worthless. Some say that prosperity is gained only by marrying that girl to whom one becomes attached.

When a girl reaches marriageable age, every afternoon, having dressed and adorned her becomingly, they should send her with her female friends to attend sports activities, sacrifices and marriage ceremonies, thus showing her to society. They should also welcome those who come with their friends and relations for the purpose of marrying their daughter, with kind words and signs of friendship. On this occasion too, they should dress their daughter suitably and present her. After this they should find an auspicious day on which a decision can be made about their daughter's marriage. When the prospective groom and his family arrive, they should ask them to bathe and dine, and settle the matter after a while.

When a girl is thus acquired according to the custom of the region, or the man's desire, he should marry her in accordance with the Holy Writ, according to one of the four kinds of marriage.

Some *shlokas* elaborate this:

Interaction in society, such as completing verses begun by others, marriages, and auspicious ceremonies should be contracted neither with superiors, nor inferiors, but with our equals. A man reaches for a high connection when after marrying a girl, he has to serve her and her relations like a servant, and indeed, such a connection is censured by the noble. On the other hand, when a man, together with his relations, lord it over his wife, this a reproachable situation and is looked upon as a low connection by the wise. But when both the man and the woman afford mutual pleasure to each other, and when the relatives on both sides pay respect to one another, this is a connection in the proper sense of the word. Therefore a man should contract neither a high connection by which he is obliged to bow down afterwards, nor a low connection, which is universally reprehended by all.

Krishna takes the opportunity and play with Radha's breasts as she shies away. (Pages 136-137) The marriage of Shiva and Parvati or Meenakshi, fish-eyed goddess is accorded the highest form of marriage, prajapatya, royal marriage. It is celebrated in the great Meenakshi temple in an annual festival celebrated in their honor.

INSTILLING CONFIDENCE
IN THE bRidE

कन्याविस्त्रंभण प्रकरण

Kanyavistrambhana Prakarana

or the first three days after marriage, the girl and her husband should sleep on the floor, abstain from sexual pleasures, and eat food without seasoning it with either alkali or salt. For the next seven days they should bathe amidst the sounds of auspicious musical instruments, adorn themselves, dine together, and pay attention to their relations and other guests who have come to witness their marriage. This applies to persons of all castes.

Tender Beginnings

On the tenth night the man should commence gentle love-play with soft words, thus winning the girl's confidence. Some say that to win her over, the man should not speak to her for three days, but the followers of Babhravya opine that the girl may be discouraged by seeing him spiritless like a pillar, become dejected, and begin to despise him. Vatsyayana, however, maintains that though the man

should begin to win her over and inspire her confidence, he should abstain from sexual pleasures straightaway.

Being of a tender nature, women desire gentle beginnings, and if forcibly approached by men with whom they are only slightly acquainted, they can become fearful of a sexual relationship, and may even become male haters. The man should therefore approach the girl according to her liking, and employ those devices by which he may be able to inspire her confidence.

He should start by embracing her with the upper part of his body because that is easier and simpler. If the girl is grown up, or if the man has known her for some time, he may embrace her in lamplight, but if he is not well acquainted with her, or if she is a young girl, he should embrace her in darkness.

If the girl accepts the embrace, he should put a *tambula,* screw of betel nut and betel leaves, in her mouth, and if she does not take it, he should persuade her with conciliatory words, entreaties, oaths and kneeling at her feet, for it is a universal rule that however bashful or angry a woman may be, she never disregards a man kneeling at her feet. He should then give her the *tambula* and kiss her mouth softly and gracefully. When she has been won over, he should ask her about things he knows about, or pretends to know nothing of, and which can be answered in a few words. If she does not reply, he should ask her repeatedly in a conciliatory manner. If she still does not speak, he should urge her to reply because, as Ghotakamukha says, " girls hear everything said to them by men, but may not sometimes say a single word".

When she is thus importuned, the girl should reply by shaking her head, but if she has quarreled with the man, she should not do even

---

(Left) When a boy begins to woo the girl he loves he should spend time with her, amusing her with gifts and games as may be agreeable to the girl's disposition.

that. When asked by him whether she desires him and likes him, she should remain silent for a long while, and when at last importuned to reply, should give him a favorable answer by a nod of her head. If the man is previously unacquainted with the girl, he should converse with her via a female friend who is in the confidence of both, and can carry on the conversation for both sides. On such an occasion the girl should smile with her head bent down, and if the female friend says more on her part than meant to, she should chide her. The female friend should comment in jest even what she is not asked to by the girl, by saying, "She says so", on which the girl should say indistinctly and prettily, "Oh no! I did not say so", and then smile and throw an occasional glance towards the man.

Winning Her Over

If the girl is familiar with the man, she should place near him

silently, the *tambula*, the ointment, or the garland that he may have asked for, or she may tie them up in his upper garment. While she is engaged in this, the man should touch her young breasts by pressing with the nails, and if she prevents him from doing so, he

should say, "I will not do it again if you will embrace me", and in this way make her embrace him. During the embrace he should repeatedly stroke her body with his hands, then place her in his lap and try to gain her consent. If she does not yield, he should startle her by saying, "I shall impress marks of my teeth and nails on your lips and breasts, and then make similar marks on my own body, and tell my friends that you made them. What will you do then?" In this and other ways, as trust and confidence are created in the minds of children, so should the man win her over to his wishes. After her confidence has increased, he should feel her whole body with his hands and kiss her all over; if he presses her thighs with his hands and she does not discourage him, he should caress the joints of her thighs. If she tries to prevent him he should ask her, "What harm is there in doing it?" and persuade her to let him continue. After this he should touch her private parts, loosen her girdle and the knot of her dress, and turning up her lower garment, stroke the joints of her naked thighs. In fact he should do all this under various pretenses, but not actually begin the sexual act. Only then should he he teach her the sixty-four arts, tell her how much he loves her, and describe to her the hopes which he fervently entertains about her. He should also promise to be faithful to her, and dispel all her fears with respect to rival women. At last, when she has finally

A girl forcibly enjoyed by one who does not understand the female psyche becomes nervous and dejected, and begins to fear the man. Later, when her love is not understood or returned, she sinks into despondency, and becomes either a hater of mankind altogether, or hating her own man, takes recourse to relationships with other men.

(Left) This wooden panel shows lovers in various erotic poses. Such objects were much in vogue those days and were often shown by young men to their sweethearts to arouse sexual desire in them.

overcome her bashfulness, he should begin to enjoy her in such a way as to delight her.

Some *shlokas* state:

A man acting according to the inclinations of a girl, should try and win her over so that she may love him and place her confidence in him. The man who either implicitly follows the inclination of a girl, or wholly opposes her, cannot succeed, and should, therefore, adopt a middle course. He who knows how to make himself beloved to women, to respect their honor and create confidence in them, becomes deserving of their love. But he who neglects a girl, thinking she is too bashful, is despised by her as a beast ignorant of the working of the female mind. Moreover, a girl forcibly enjoyed by one who does not understand the female psyche becomes nervous, uneasy and dejected, and begins to fear the man who has taken advantage of her. Later, when her love is neither understood nor returned, she sinks into despondency, and becomes either a hater of mankind altogether, or hating her own man, takes recourse to relationships with other men.

The heroine's maids stand at the doorstep waiting to be the first one to announce the arrival of her handsome hero for whom she longs. (Right) Under a bower of mango fruits, the nayika curves seductively — an alluring sight for any youthful lover.

COURTING A MAID

बालोपक्रमण प्रकरण

Balopakramana Prakarana

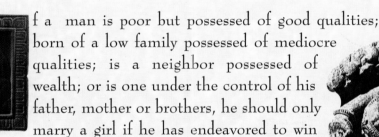

f a man is poor but possessed of good qualities; born of a low family possessed of mediocre qualities; is a neighbor possessed of wealth; or is one under the control of his father, mother or brothers, he should only marry a girl if he has endeavored to win her love and respect from her childhood itself. A boy separated from his parents and living in his maternal uncle's house, should try to win over his daughter, or some other girl, even though she may have been previously betrothed to another. This way of winning over a girl, says Ghotakamukha, is unexceptional, because *dharma* can be accomplished by this as well as by any other way of marriage.

The Wooing Game

When a boy begins to woo the girl he loves, he should spend time with her, amusing her with pastimes fit for their age and acquaintanceship, such as picking and collecting flowers, making garlands with them, role-playing as members of a

fictitious family, cooking food, playing dice or cards, games of odds and evens, finding the middle finger, six pebbles, and other games as may be prevalent in the region and agreeable to the girl's disposition. He can also suggest amusing group games such as hide and seek, playing with seeds, hiding things in small heaps of wheat and finding them, blind man's buff, gymnastic exercises, and games which can be played with her friends and female attendants. He should also show great kindness to any woman whom the girl trusts and make new acquaintances. Above all he should befriend the daughter of the girl's nurse with kindness and little services, for if she is won over, she will not cause any obstruction even though she knows of his design. In fact sometimes she may even be able to effect a union between him and the girl. And though she may be aware of his weaknesses, she will then always extol his many excellent qualities to the girl's parents and relations, even though she may not have been asked to do so.

Presenting Her with Gifts

In these ways the man should do whatever the girl takes most delight in, and should procure for her whatever she may wish to possess, including playthings as may be hardly known to other girls. He should get her a ball dyed with various colors, and other similar curiosities; dolls made of cloth, wood, buffalo-horn, ivory, wax, flour, or earth; utensils for cooking; wooden figures such as those of a standing man and woman, a pair of rams, goats, or sheep; temples made of earth, bamboo, or wood, dedicated to various goddesses; cages for parrots, cuckoos, starlings, quails, cocks and partridges; water-vessels of different sorts and elegant forms, machines for throwing water about; lyres; stands for displaying images, stools; lac; red arsenic, yellow ointment, vermilion and collyrium, as well as sandalwood, saffron, betel nut and betel leaves. He should present these to her at different times whenever he gets

(Left) Baths in rivers, festivals, celebrations and social gatherings provide enough opportunities for young adolescent girls to seek out handsome lovers.

to meet her: some of them should be given in private, some in public, according to circumstances. In short, he should make every effort to make her look upon him as one who would do anything that she wants.

In the next phase he should get her to meet him privately, explaining that the reason for giving her presents in secret was his fear of their parents' displeasure. He can add that his gifts had been much desired by other girls. When her love shows signs of increasing he should tell her agreeable stories if she is interested in them. If she enjoys legerdemain, he should amaze her by performing tricks of jugglery; if she is curious to see a performance of the arts, he should show his own skill in them; and if she likes singing he should entertain her with music. Whenever they visit moonlight fairs and festivals, or on her return after an absence from home, he should present her with bouquets of flowers, chaplets for the head, ear ornaments and rings.

He should also teach the daughter of the girl's nurse all the sixty-four means of pleasure practiced by men, and under this pretext inform her of his great skill in the art of sexual enjoyment. He should always dress well and look good, for young women love that in their men. It is not correct to say that though

The attractive nayika examines her magnetism as she prepares for a rendezvous with her paramour. (Left) The bride's maids accompany and lead the young shy virgin bride to her husband's chamber on the nuptial night.

women may fall in love, they make no effort themselves to win over the man of their affections.

Responding with Love

A girl always shows her love through signs and actions when her lover is nearby. She never looks directly at him, becoming abashed when he looks at her; she shows her limbs to him under some pretext; looks secretly at him even when he is no longer by her side; hangs down her head when she is asked a question by him, answering indistinctly in unfinished sentences; delights being in his company for a long time; speaks to her attendants in a peculiar tone, hoping to attract his attention when he is far away; does not wish to leave the place where he is; makes him look at different things under some pretext; narrates tales to him slowly so that she may continue conversing with him for a long time; kisses and embraces a child sitting in her lap in front of him; draws ornamental marks on her female servants' foreheads; performs sportive and graceful movements when her attendants speak jestingly to her in her lover's presence; confides in her lover's friends, and respects and obeys them; shows kindness to his servants, converses with them, gives them tasks to do as if she were their mistress, and listens attentively when they relate stories about her lover to somebody else; enters his house when induced to do so by her nurse's daughter, and with her assistance manages to converse and play with him; avoids being seen by her lover when she is not well dressed and adorned; sends him her ear ornaments, a ring or garland of flowers that he may have asked for through her friend; always wears whatever he has presented her with; and becomes dejected if another prospective bridegroom is mentioned by her parents, refusing to mix with anyone from his group or with anyone who encourages his proposal.

(Left) For the first few days of marriage the couple should abstain from sexual pleasures. Gradually the man should commence gentle love play and only when her bride is totally relaxed and unafraid, should he commence the actual act.

Some *shlokas* state:

A man who has seen and perceived the feelings of the girl towards him, and who has noticed the outward signs and movements by which those feelings are expressed, should do everything in his power to effect a union with her. He should win over a young girl by childlike sports, a damsel come of age by his skill in the arts, and a young girl who loves him by recoursing to persons in whom she confides.

Behavior of the couple

एकपुरुषाभियोग प्रकरण

Ekapurushabhiyoga Prakarana

 hen a girl begins to show her love by outward signs and motions, the lover should try to win her over entirely by various means.

Strengthening Affection

When engaged with her in any game, he should intentionally hold her hand. He should practice the various kinds of embraces, such as the touching embrace, rubbing and pressing, on her. He can also show her a pair of human beings cut out of the leaf of a tree and similar objects. If engaged in water sports, he should dive at a distance from her and come up near her.

He should describe to her the pangs he suffers on her account and the beautiful dream he has had with reference to other women. At parties and assemblies of his caste he should sit near her and touch her under some pretence, and having placed his foot upon her's, should slowly touch each of her toes, pressing the ends of her nails. If successful, he should hold her foot with his hand and repeat the same thing. He should also press her finger between his toes when she happens to be washing his feet; and whenever he gives or takes anything to and from her, he should show her how much he loves her by his manners and look.

Convincing Her

He should sprinkle on her the water brought for rinsing his mouth; and when alone with her in a secluded place, or in darkness, should make love to her and tell her the true state of his mind without distressing her in any way.

Whenever he sits with her on the same seat or bed he should say, "I have something to tell you in private", and when she comes to him in a quiet place, he should express his love for her more by manner and signs than words. When he comes to know of her feelings towards him, he should pretend to be ill, and thus make

When a girl begins to show her love by her signs and motions, the lover should try to win her over entirely by practicing various kinds of embraces. He should intentionally hold her hand and praise her beauteous charms.

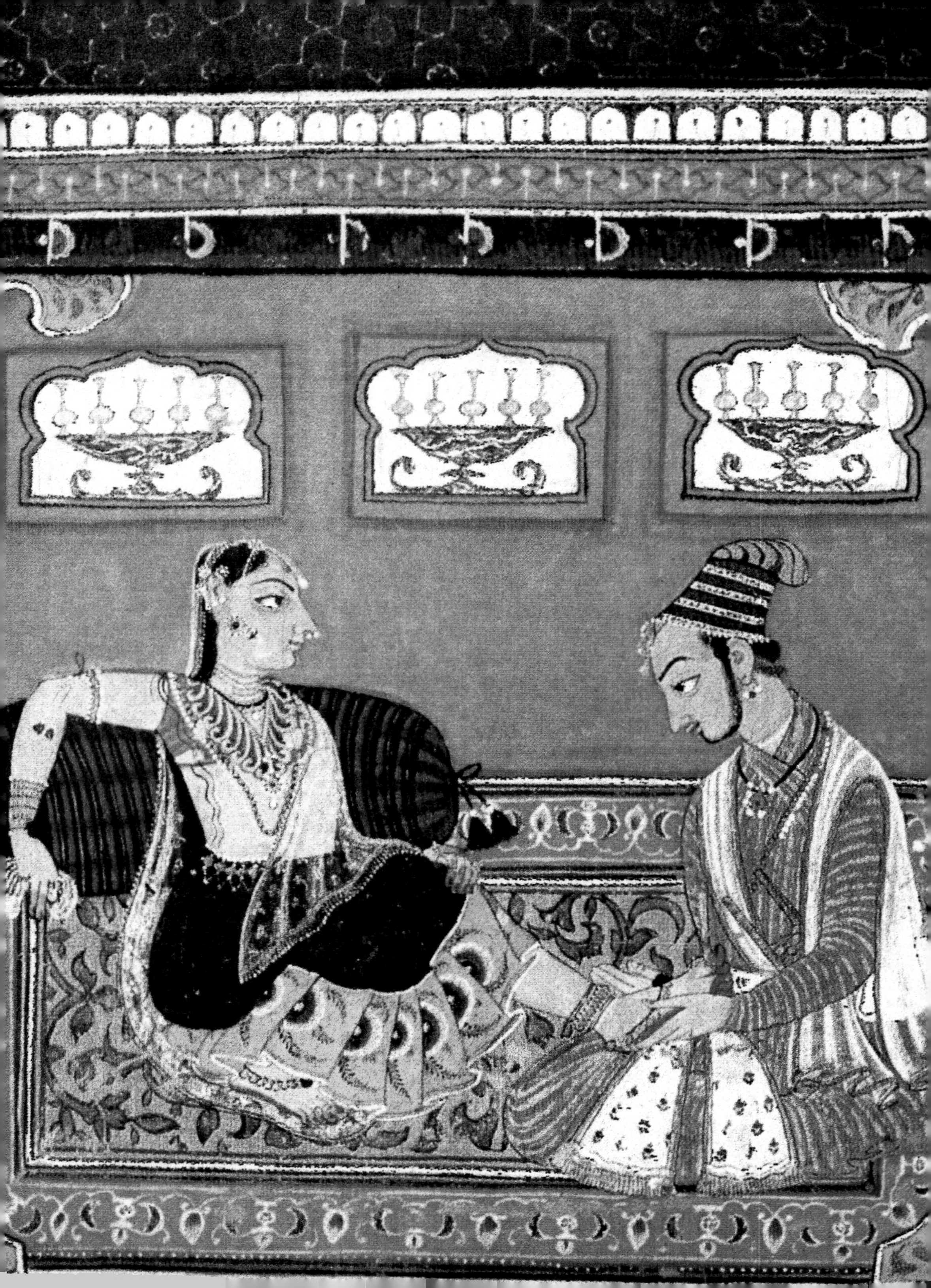

her come to his house to meet him. There he should intentionally hold her hand and place it on his eyes and forehead, and under the pretence of preparing some medicine, ask her to do it for him with the following words: "This must be done by you, and by nobody else". When she wants to leave he should let her go, with an earnest request to visit him again. This ruse of illness should be continued for three days and three nights. After this, when she begins coming to see him frequently, he should carry on long conversations with her, for says Ghotakamukha, "Though a man loves a girl ever so much, he never succeeds in winning her without a great deal of talking". Only when he discovers that he has completely won her over, he may then begin to enjoy her. The belief that women grow less timid during the evening and in darkness, and are desirous of congress themselves at those times, and should, therefore, be enjoyed at those hours, is only a fallacy.

When it is impossible for the man to carry on his endeavors alone, he should take the help of the nurse's daughter or a female friend in whom she confides, and arrange for the girl to be brought to him without making his designs known to her. Then he can woo her. Or, he may send his own female servant to live with the girl as her friend, with the intent of winning her over.

At last, when he knows the state of her feelings by her outward manner and conduct towards him at religious festivals, marriage ceremonies, fairs, theatres, public assemblies, and similar occasions, he should begin to enjoy her when she is alone, for Vatsyayana maintains that women, when resorted to at proper times and in proper places, do not turn away from their lovers.

Winning over a Male

When a girl possesses good qualities and is well bred, even though she is born in a humble family or does not have any wealth, and is,

---

(Pages 152-153) The lover should describe to her the pangs he suffers on her account and the beautiful dream he had of her. He should sit near her and touch her under some pretense. (Left) He should slowly touch her toes, pressing the ends of her nails. All this and his mannerisms and his look will show her how much he loves her.

therefore, not desired by her equals; or is an orphan deprived of her parents, but observing the rules of her family and caste, wishes to get married when she comes of age, she should endeavor to win over a strong and good-looking young man, or a man whom she thinks will marry her on account of having a weak mind, even without the consent of his parents. She must achieve this by endearing herself to the young man, and meeting him frequently. Her mother may also arrange for them to meet often through her female friends and her nurse's daughter. The girl herself can try to be alone with her beloved in a quiet place, and give him flowers, betel nuts, betel leaves and perfumes. She should show him her skill in the arts of massaging, scratching and pressing with the nails. She should also talk to him on subjects he likes.

But the ancients say that however much a girl loves a man, she should not offer herself to him or make the first overtures, for she would lose her dignity and could be scorned and rejected. But when the man expresses his wish to enjoy her, she should be favorable to him, showing no change in her demeanor when he embraces her, and receive all the manifestations of his love as if she were ignorant of the state of his mind. But when he tries to kiss her she should oppose him; when he begs to have sexual intercourse with her, she should only let him touch her private parts, and that too with considerable difficulty; and though importuned by him, not yield to him as if of her own accord, but resist his attempts to have her. It is only when she is certain that she is truly loved and that her lover is indeed devoted to her and will not change his mind, that she should give herself up to

A girl who is much sought after should marry the man that she likes, and who she thinks would be obedient to her, and capable of giving her pleasure. A husband who is obedient but master of himself, even though poor and not good looking, is better than one who is common to many women, even though he is handsome.

(Right) The divine couple, Shiva and Parvati, seated on Nandi bull.

him and persuade him to marry her quickly. After losing her virginity she should tell her confidantes about it. Some *shlokas* on the topic state:

A girl who is much sought after should marry the man that she likes, and who she thinks would be obedient to her, and capable of giving her pleasure. But when due to the desire of wealth, a girl is married by her parents to a rich man without taking into consideration the character or looks of the bridegroom; or when given to a man who has several wives, she never becomes attached to him, even though he may be endowed with good qualities, is obedient to her will, active, strong, healthy, and is anxious to please her in every way. A husband who is obedient but master of

himself, even though poor and not good looking, is better than one who is common to many women, even though he is handsome and attractive. The wives of rich men who have several wives, are not generally attached to their husbands, and do not confide in them, and though they possess all the external enjoyments of life, they still take recourse to other men.

A man who is of a low mind, who has fallen from his social position, an old man, or a man who is much given to traveling, does not deserve to be married; neither does one who has many wives and children, nor one who is devoted to sports and gambling, and who comes to his wife only when he likes. Of all the lovers of a girl he alone is her true husband who possesses the qualities that are liked by her, and only such a husband enjoys real superiority over her, because he is the husband of love.

Kinds of MARRIAGE

विवाहयोग प्रकरण

Vivahayoga Prakarana

When a girl cannot meet her lover frequently in private, she may send her nurse's daughter to him, it being understood that she has confidence in her and the latter will act in her interests.

The Nurse's Daughter

On meeting the man, the nurse's daughter should tell him about the noble birth, good disposition, beauty, talent, skill, knowledge of human nature, and affection of the girl without letting him suppose that she has been sent by the girl to win over the man's heart. She may also praise the excellent qualities of the man to the girl, especially those which she knows would please her. She should speak with disparagement of the girl's other lovers, the avarice and indiscretion of their parents, and the fickleness of their relations. She may also quote examples of girls of ancient times such as Shakuntala who, having united with lovers of their own caste and choice, were happy ever afterwards. And she should also

(Left) The maids prepare the bride for her first night. The moment is filled with laughter and song as they apply henna, rouge, collyrium and perfume to the anxious girl.

tell of other girls who married into great families and troubled by rival wives, became wretched and miserable, and were finally abandoned. She should speak of the good fortune, continual happiness, chastity, obedience and affection of the man, and if the girl becomes amorous about him, should endeavor to allay the shame, fear and suspicions about any disaster that might result from her marriage. In brief, she should enact the complete role of a female messenger by telling the girl about the man's affection for her, the places he frequents, and the endeavors he is making to meet her, by frequently repeating, "It will be all right if the man takes you away forcibly and unexpectedly".

The *Gandharva* Marriage

When the girl is won over and acts openly with the man as his wife, he should have fire brought from the house of a Brahmin, and spreading the *kusha*, grass, upon the ground, and offering oblation to the fire, he should marry her according to the precepts of religious law. After this he should inform his parents of the fact, because in the opinion of ancient authors, a marriage solemnly contracted in the presence of fire, cannot afterwards be set aside.

After the consummation of the marriage, the man's relations should be acquainted with the bond. The girl's relations should also be apprised of it in such a way that they consent to the marriage and overlook the manner in which it was brought about. In fact they should be appeased with presents given affectionately and favorable conduct. In this manner the man would have married the girl according to the *Gandharva* form of marriage.

Forced Marriage

When the girl is indecisive, or does not express her readiness to marry, the man can get her in one of the following ways:

On a fitting occasion and under some ruse, he may, with the help of a female friend whom he can trust, and who is also well known to the girl's family, have the girl brought unexpectedly to his house. He should then bring fire from the house of a Brahmin, and proceed as suggested above.

When the marriage of the girl with some other person draws near, the man should disparage the future husband to the utmost to the girl's mother, and then having persuaded the girl to come with her mother's consent to a neighboring house, he should bring fire from the house of a Brahmin, and make her his wife.

The man should become a great friend of the girl's brother who is his own age, and is addicted to courtesans and intrigues with the wives of other men. He should assist the brother in such matters and give him occasional presents. Having won him over, he should then tell him about his great love for his sister, as young men sacrifice even their own lives for the sake of those who may be of the same age, and

---

Maids play melodious music during a wedding ceremony. (Left) Radha and Krishna enjoy the attention of their devotees during a boat ride.

possess the same habits and disposition as themselves. After this the brother should assist in bringing the girl to a secure place, bring fire from the house of a Brahmin, and enjoin her in marriage.

On a festive occasion the man can get the nurse's daughter to give the girl some intoxicating substance and then have her brought to a secret place. He can then enjoy her before she recovers from her intoxication, bring fire from the house of a Brahmin, and make her his wife.

With the connivance of the nurse's daughter, he can carry off the girl from her house while she is asleep, enjoy her before she recovers from her sleep, bring fire from the house of a Brahmin, and induce her into wedlock.

Or when the girl goes to a garden or to a village in the neighborhood, the man and his friends can fall on her guards and have them killed or frightened away. He can then abduct and forcibly marry her.

There are *shlokas* that say:

In all the forms of marriage described in this work, the one that precedes is better than the one that follows it on account of its being more in accordance with the commands of religion, and therefore it is only when it is impossible to carry out the former that the latter should be resorted to. As the fruit of all good marriages is love, the Gandharva *form of marriage is respected, even though it is formed under unfavorable circumstances, because it fulfills the object sought for. Another cause of the respect accorded to the* Gandharva *form of marriage is that it brings forth happiness, causes less trouble in its performance than the other forms of marriage, and is, above all, the result of previous love.*

(Left) Frustrated , the young couple decide to elope. In a bold move the hero steals up next to the wall besides his heroine's chamber on elephant back. The girl ready, eager and waiting , abetted by her maid climbs down into her lover's arms as they vanish away into the darkness of the night. (Pages 162-163) When a girl of the same caste is married in accordance with the prevalent local customs and the Holy writ in presence of a Brahmin, priest and by making offerings to the holy fire it ensures happiness in the couple's life and lasts for ever.

The Wife

Duties of a wife

Senior and junior wives

BOOK 4

Duties of a wife

एकचारिणीवृत्त प्रकरण

Ekacharinivritta Prakarana

 virtuous woman, who has affection for her husband, should act in conformity with his wishes as if he were a divine being, and with his consent take upon herself the care of his family. The house should be well cleaned, the floor smooth and polished, and decorated with flowers to make it neat and becoming.

Beautification with a Garden

She should surround the house with a garden, and place in it all the materials required for the morning, noon and evening sacrifices. She should revere the sanctuary of the household gods, for, says Gonardiya, "Nothing so much attracts the heart of a householder to his wife as a careful observance of the household rituals".

In the kitchen garden, usually at the rear of the house, she should plant beds of green vegetables, sugar-cane, cummin seeds, fig trees, mustard, parsley, soya and bay leaf.

She may plan a flower garden in front of the house with *kubjyaka,*

(Left) A mid-18th century Kishengarh wall hanging depicting Krishna and Radha in the throes of divine passion.

amalaka, mallika, tagara, kurantaka, navamallika, nandavarata and *japa* trees, jasmine trees, and yellow amaranth; plantations of *balaka and ushiraka*. The garden can be beautified with marble seats arranged in arbors, constructed as restful places to enjoy peace and quiet; a diviner should find a source of water and a well to provide water for drinking and bathing, as also to fill a tank or pool.

Behavior and Etiquette

The wife should always avoid the company of women who are beggars, *bhikshunis,* mendicants, unchaste and roguish, fortune tellers and witches. As regards meals she should always consider her husband's likes and dislikes and the foods that are good or injurious for him. When she hears his footsteps coming home she should rise immediately and be ready to do as he bids, and either order her female servant to wash his feet, or wash them herself. When going anywhere with him, she should wear her ornaments. Without his consent she should neither give nor accept invitations, attend marriages and sacrifices, mix with female friends, visit temples or engage in any games. She should sit down after him, get up before him, and never awaken him when he is asleep. The kitchen should be situated in a quiet and secluded corner, inaccessible to strangers, and always kept clean and free of dirt and pests.

If her husband misbehaves, she should not blame him excessively, even though she may be a little displeased. She should not use

The two young maids assist the wife in delivering a healthy baby boy. Failure to deliver a heir can lead the man to go in for another wife. (Right) A woman who is of a noble family and leads a chaste life , devoted to her husband , and bears him a male heir acquires dharma, artha, kama *and obtains a high position.*

abusive language towards him, but rebuke him with conciliatory words, whether he is with friends or alone. Moreover, she should not be a nag, for, says Gonardiya, "There is no cause of dislike on the part of a husband so great as this characteristic in a wife". She should also avoid giving sulky looks, speaking aside, standing in the doorway and looking at passers-by, conversing in the pleasure groves, and remaining in a lonely place for a long time; and finally she should always keep her body, teeth, hair and everything belonging to her tidy, sweet, dainty and clean.

When the wife wants to approach her husband in private she should wear colored clothes, ornaments and flowers, and some sweet-smelling ointments or unguents. But her everyday dress should consist of a thin, close-textured cloth, a few ornaments and flowers, and a little scent. She should also observe the fasts and vows of her husband, and when he tries to prevent her, she should persuade him to let her do it.

Supervising the Household

At appropriate times of the year, when they happen to be in plenty and therefore cheap, the housewife should purchase and stock useful articles like earthen pots, cane baskets, wooden cups and bowls, and iron and copper vessels to guard against rising prices. She should be careful to ensure that supplies of all items of common use such as rock salt, oils, perfumes, pepper, medicines, rare drugs and spices are stored in the house to cater for possible scarcity. In the garden shed should be kept the seeds of radish, potatoes, beet, spinach, *damanka,* cucumber, *gonikarika,* garlic, and onion, which have been collected from season to season, to be sown at the proper time.

The wife should not disclose to strangers the amount of her wealth, or the secrets which her

husband has confided in her. She should surpass all the women who are her peers in cleverness, appearance, knowledge of cookery, pride, and manner of serving the husband.

All sales and purchases of household goods and chattels should be well attended to. Income should be increased and expenditure reduced as far as possible. Milk that is not consumed should be turned into *ghee* or clarified butter. Oil and sugar should be prepared at home; spinning and weaving should also be done there; and a stock of ropes and cords, and barks of trees for twisting into ropes should be kept. The pounding of rice should be carefully supervised, and the residue of small grain and chaff should be used. The wife should always be shrewd and careful with money, regular in paying all dues, in particular the salaries of servants, and other household expenses. Her additional duties include looking after the tilling of the fields; the flocks and herds; the making and repairing of farm equipage; the care of domestic animals and pets such as rams, cocks, quail, parrots, starlings, cuckoos, peacocks, monkeys, and deer, and finally reconciling the income and expenditure of the day.

The good housewife is liberal and understanding towards her servants, and reward them on holidays and festivals but does not give away anything without informing her husband.

Worn-out clothes should be given to those servants who have done good work, to show them that their services have been appreciated, or used for other purposes. The vessels in which wine is prepared and kept, should be carefully looked after, and put away for use at the proper time.

Honoring Friends of Her Husband and In-laws

She would welcome her husband's friends with flowers, perfumes, incense, betel leaves, and betel nut.

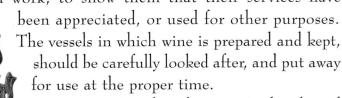

She should treat her parents-in-law with the respect that they deserve, always remain dependent on their will, never contradict them, speak to them in few and gentle words, not laugh loudly in their presence, and act with their friends and enemies as with her own. In addition she should not be vain, or too taken up with her enjoyments.

During the absence of her husband on a journey, the virtuous woman should wear only her auspicious ornaments, and observe fasts and feasts in honor of the gods. While anxious for news of her husband, she should continue to look after her household affairs. She should sleep near the older women of the house, and make herself agreeable to them. She should look after the things that her husband likes, and continue the works that have been begun by him. She should not visit her relations except on occasions of joy and sorrow, go in her usual traveling dress, accompanied by her husband's servants, and not stay there long. And when her husband returns from his journey, she should receive him at first in her ordinary clothes, to make him aware of she has lived during his absence, and giving him some presents, with materials for the worship of the deity.

Some *shlokas* state this:

The wife, whether she be a woman of noble family, or a virgin, widow remarried, or a concubine, should lead a chaste life, devoted to her husband, and doing everything for his welfare. Women acting thus acquire dharma, artha, *and* kama, *obtain a high position, and generally keep their husbands devoted to them.*

A virtuous woman, who has affection for her husband should act in conformity with his wishes, as if he were a divine being. (Left) Shiva and Parvati in an amorous embrace. The bronze sculpture has Tantric origins.

राजा नोल भा श्रावी पुद्धे छे ज
र

SENIOR ANd jUNiOR WiVES

ज्येष्ठादिवृत्त प्रकरण

Jyeshtadivritta Prakarana

I f a husband remarries during his wife's lifetime, the causes are: her folly or ill-temper, her husband's dislike of her, the want of offspring, the continual birth of daughters, and the incontinence of the husband.

Behavior towards Other Wives

From the very beginning, a wife should endeavor to win over her husband's heart by her continual devotion, good temper, and wisdom. If, however, she bears him no children, she should tell her husband to marry another woman. And when the second wife is brought to the house, she should give the latter a position superior to her own, and look upon her as a sister. In the morning she should forcibly make her adorn herself in their husband's presence, and not object to him favoring her. If the younger wife does anything to displease their husband, the elder

(Left) A man marrying many wives should act fairly towards all of them. He should give each of them a place and respect as may suit the occasion and should not reveal to one wife , the love, passion and confidential reproaches of the other. (Following page) A woman who is good natured and takes care of her husband wins her husband's attachments and obtains superiority over her rivals.

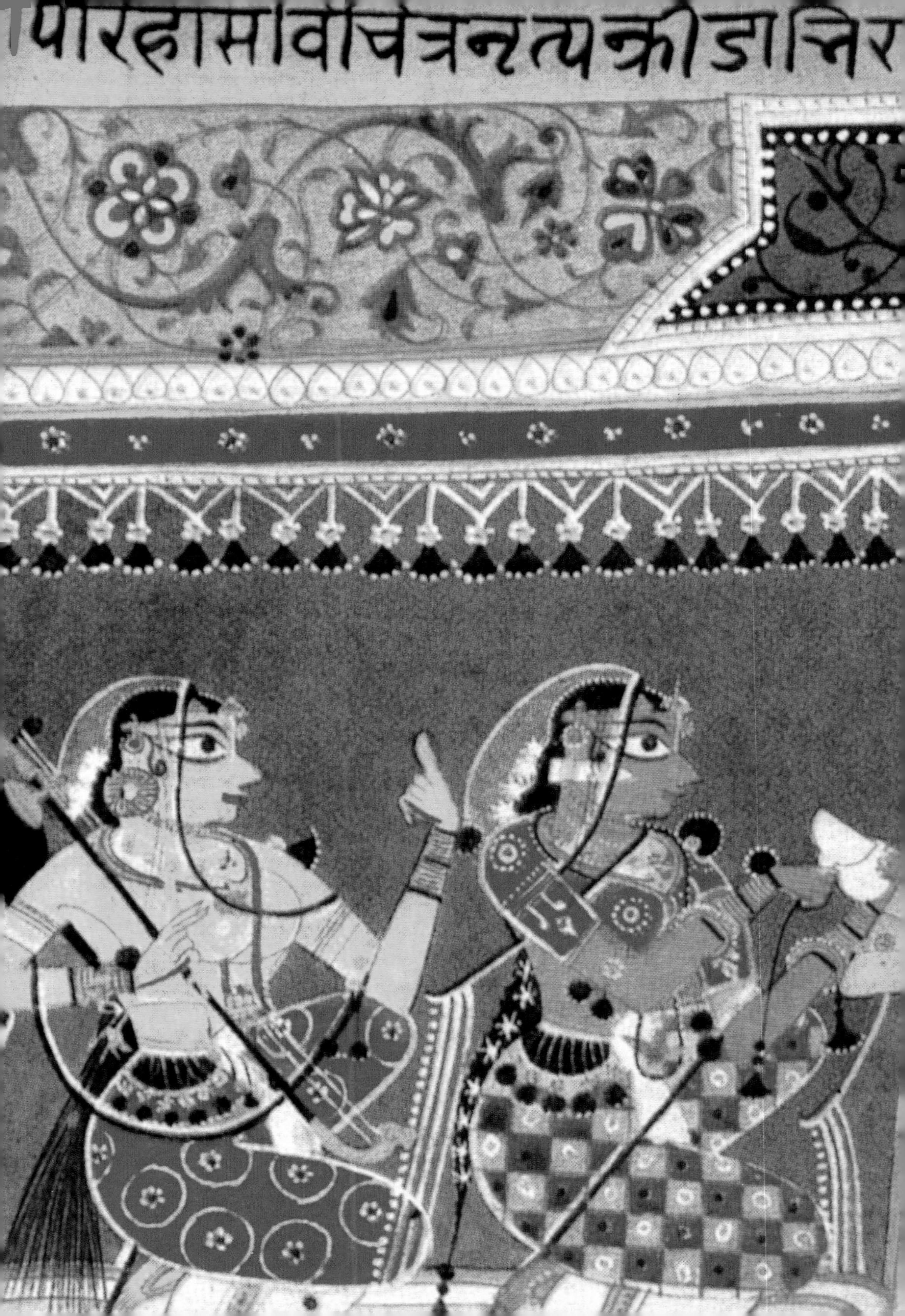

इवजा तुमदीजव

चंपावती

विद्वुन:

one should be ready to give her careful advice, and teach her various ways to please him. She should treat the younger wife's children as her own, give her attendants more regard than her own, cherish her friends with love and kindness, and her relations with great honor.

When there are several other wives besides herself, the elder wife should associate with the one immediately next to her in rank and age, and instigate the wife who has recently enjoyed her husband's favor to quarrel with the present favorite. She should sympathize with the former, and having collected all the other wives together, get them to denounce the favorite as a scheming and wicked woman, without however committing herself in any way. If the favorite wife happens to quarrel with the husband, then the elder wife should take her side and give her false encouragement, and thus actually cause the quarrel to intensify. If there is only a small quarrel, the elder wife should do all she can to work it up into a large one. But if after all this she finds that the husband still continues to love his favorite wife, she should change her tactics, and endeavor to bring about a conciliation between them, so as to avoid her husband's displeasure.

The younger wife should regard the elder wife as her mother, and not give away anything, even to her own relations, without the elder's knowledge. She should tell the elder everything about herself, and not approach her husband without her permission. She should not reveal whatever the senior wife tells her, and look after her children more than her own. When alone with her husband

The lovers seem to be distracted during their passionate love game.(Left) The loving husband showers his affection on his favorite wife by offering her a goblet of wine.

she should serve him well, without sharing the pain she suffers due to a rival's existence. She may obtain from her husband some marks of his particular regard for her, tell him that she lives only for him, and for the regard that he has for her.

She should never reveal her love for her husband, nor his for her to any person, either in pride or in anger, for a wife who reveals her husband's secrets is despised by him. As for seeking to obtain the regard of her husband, Gonardiya says that the regard of her husband should always be sought in private, for fear of the elder wife. If the elder wife is disliked by her husband, or is childless, the junior should sympathize with her, and ask her husband to do the same, but should surpass her in leading the life of a chaste woman.

Remarriage of Widows

A widow in poor circumstances, or of a weak nature, and who allies herself again to a man, is called a widow remarried. In Babhravya's view a virgin widow should not marry a man of bad character or poor

qualities whom she may have to leave and then take recourse to another person. Gonardiya feels that since a widow remarries for happiness, which is secured by the possession of excellent qualities in her husband, joined to love of enjoyment, it is better to find a man endowed with such qualities in the first instance. Vatsyayana however thinks that a widow may marry any person that she likes, and whom she thinks will suit her.

At the time of her marriage the widow should obtain sufficient money from her husband to pay for drinking parties, picnics with her relations, and gifts for them and her friends; or she may prefer to do these things at her own cost. Similarly she may wear either the ornaments given by her husband or her own. But there is no fixed rule about the presents exchanged mutually with affection between her husband and herself. If she leaves her husband after marriage, she should return whatever he may have given her, with the exception of mutual presents. If however she is driven out of the house by her husband, she should not return anything to him.

After her marriage she should live in her husband's house like one of the chief members of the family, but should treat the other ladies of the family with kindness, the servants with generosity, and all the friends of the house with familiarity and good temper. She should show that she is better acquainted with the sixty-four arts than the other ladies of the house, and in any quarrels with her husband, she

The younger wife should always respect the elder and should not do anything without her knowledge. (Left) A woman adept in the sixty four arts of pleasure is sure to become her husband's favorite. Here she encircles her legs around his back and pushes him forward to provide for an extra thrust , while he plays with her breasts.

should not rebuke him severely but in private do everything that he wishes, making use of the sixty-four ways of enjoyment. She should be obliging to her husband's other wives, give presents to their children, behave as their mistress, and make ornaments and playthings for them. She should confide more in her husband's friends and servants than in his other wives, and finally she should enjoy drinking parties, picnics, fairs and festivals, and all kinds of games and amusements.

The Neglected Wife

A woman who is disliked by her husband, and annoyed and distressed by his other wives, should associate with his favorite wife who serves him more than the others, and should teach her all the arts with which she is acquainted. She should act as the nurse of her husband's children, and having won over his friends, should through them make him aware of her devotion to him. In religious ceremonies she should be a leader, as also in vows and fasts, and should not be too conceited. When her husband is lying on his bed she should only go near him when it is agreeable to him; she should never rebuke him or show obstinacy in any way. If her husband quarrels with any of his other wives, she should reconcile them, and if he desires to see any woman secretly, she should arrange a

The junior and senior wives should live together in harmony participating in all religious and social events of the household. (Right) An old peasant passing by seems delighted by the charms of a beautiful maiden and stops to admire her. A virtuous wife should not stand outside the house or on the doorstep as it is construed as an invitation by desperate seeking males.

meeting between them. Making herself acquainted with his weaknesses, she should keep them secret, and behave in such a way that he may look upon her as a devoted wife.

Conduct of the King and the Royal Ladies

The female attendants in the inner court called *kanchukiyas* and *mahattarikas,* may bring flowers, ointments and clothes from the king's wives to him, and he should give them as presents to the servants, along with the things worn by him the previous day. In the afternoon the king, having dressed and put on his ornaments, should interview the women of the harem, who should also be dressed and decorated with jewels. Then having given to each of them a place and respect as may suit the occasion and as they may deserve, he should carry on a cheerful conversation with them. After that he should meet his wives who are virgin widows remarried, and then, the concubines and dancing girls. All of them should be visited in their own private rooms.

When the king rises from his noonday sleep, the female attendant on duty should come to him accompanied by the female attendants of the wife whose turn it is to spend the night with him, and of her who may have been accidentally passed over as her turn arrived, and of her who may have been unwell at the time of her turn. These attendants should place before the king the unguents sent by each of these wives, marked

with the seal of their rings, and tell him their names and their reasons for sending them. After the king accepts one of their unguents, she is then informed that she has been chosen.

At festivals, singing parties and exhibitions, all the king's wives should be treated with respect and served drinks. But the women of the harem should neither be allowed to go out alone, nor should any women from outside be allowed to enter except those whose character is well known. The king's wives should not do any work that is too fatiguing.

There are some *shlokas* on the subject:

A man marrying many wives should act fairly towards them all. He should neither disregard nor pass over their faults, and should not reveal to one wife the love, passion, bodily blemishes and confidential reproaches of the other. No opportunity should be given to any of them of speaking to him about their rivals, and if one of them does so, he should chide her and tell her that she has exactly the same blemishes in her character. He should please one by secret confidence, another by secret respect, and another by secret flattery, and he should please them all by going to gardens, amusements, presents honoring their relations, telling them secrets, and lastly by loving unions, A young woman who is of a good temper, and who conducts herself according to the precepts of the Holy Writ, wins her husband's attachments, and obtains superiority over her rivals.

The hero entraps his heroine using the strength of his thighs and pushes into her yoni. (Left) The king and his chosen wife are surrounded by female attendants of the inner court, who cheerfully converse with them and bath in the pool to make the environment ideal for a loving union, which is to follow.

Seducing the Wives of Others

Characteristics of men and women

Getting acquainted

Ascertaining emotions

Duties of a go-between

Behavior of a king

Conduct of ladies of the inner court

Book 5

CHARACTERISTICS of MEN AND WOMEN

स्त्रीपुरुष्शीलावस्थापन प्रकरण

Stripurushasheelavasthapana Prakarana

he wives of other men may be resorted to on the occasions described earlier, but their acquisition, their fitness for cohabitation, the danger in uniting with them, and the future effect of these unions, should first of all be examined.

Justification for Seducing Other Men's Wives

A man may resort to another's wife to save his own life, when he perceives that his love for her proceeds from one degree of intensity to another. There are ten degrees in number: love of the eye; attachment of the mind; constant reflection; insomnia; loss of will; emaciation of the body; turning away from pleasure and enjoyment; shameless behavior; mental imbalance; physical debility, weakness leading to vertigo, fainting fits; no will to live. Ancient sages say that a man can perceive the disposition,

(Left) When a woman gives a man an opportunity, and manifests her own love, he should proceed to enjoy her. She would make this evident by speaking to him tremblingly and exposing the erogenous parts of her body in secret places, when the opportunity occurs.

truthfulness, purity, and will of a young woman, as also the intensity or weakness of her passions, from the form of her body, and from her characteristic marks and signs. But Vatsyayana is of opinion that these are not true tests of character, and that women should be judged by their conduct, the outward expression of their thoughts, and by the movements of their bodies.

In Gonikaputra's opinion, generally a woman falls in love with every handsome man she sees, as does every man with a beautiful woman, but frequently they do not take any further steps due to various considerations. In love the following circumstances are peculiar to the woman. She loves without regard to right or wrong, and does not try to win over a man simply to achieve a particular purpose. Moreover, when a man first makes up to her she naturally shrinks from him, even though she may be willing to unite with him. But when the attempts to win her are repeated and renewed, she consents at last. However a man, even though he begins to love, conquers his feelings due to morality and wisdom, and though his thoughts are often on the woman, he does not yield, even though an attempt be made to win him over. He sometimes tries to win the object of his affections, and if he having fails, leaves her alone in the future. And when a woman is won, he often becomes indifferent about her. But to say that a man does not care for what is easily gained, and only desires a thing which cannot be obtained without difficulty, is talk.

The busy hero takes a moment off to shoot an arrow at the distracting prey. (Pages 190-191) As most girls are not acquainted with sexual union, they should be treated with delicacy, and the man should proceed with considerable caution, though in the case of women accustomed to sexual intercourse, this is not necessary. (Left) Men who generally obtain success with women are skilled in the art of love, skillful at narrating stories, acquainted with them from childhood and admired by them for their athletic prowess.

Why Women Avoid Other Men

A woman rejects the overtures of a man due to: affection for her husband and desire for lawful progeny; lack of favorable opportunity; anger at his familiarity and difference in social status; modesty at his cleverness; uncertainty because he is frequently traveling and may have another attachment; alarm at his lack of secrecy; his excessive devotion and regard for his friends; apprehension that he is not earnest; timid at his his illustrious position; fear of his strength and impetuous passion; the memory of having once lived with him on only friendly terms; disdain at his ignorance of the arts; uncertainty at his character; unhappiness at his lack of perception of her love for him; compassion at any unfortunate consequences of his passion; apprehension at her own imperfections; fear of discovery; dread that he may be employed by her husband to test her chastity, and doubt about his regard for morality.

Any obstacle perceived by the man should be removed from the very beginning. By showing great love he should allow the woman to overcome her bashfulness at his greatness or his ability. He should offset the lack of opportunity, or his inaccessibility by showing her some easy way of access. He can reduce the excessive respect she has for him by making himself very familiar. Her perception of his low character should be removed by showing his valour and his wisdom; his neglect, by extra attention; and her fear, by giving her proper encouragement.

The nayika *bends her body backwards in a yogic stance to allow deeper penetration in the standing pose. (Left) A handsome warrior has secretly entered the confines of a king's inner court and displays his sexual energy by attracting and enjoying many women at the same time.*

Successful Men

Men who generally obtain success with women are skilled in the art of love if they are well versed in all aspects of the science of love; skillful at narrating stories; acquainted with them from childhood and admired by them for their athletic prowess; send presents to them and talk fluently and elegantly; are always attentive to them; are charming and young, but innocent and inexperienced in the matters of love; aware of their weaknesses, and much sought after by women superior to them and sent to them secretly by the latter's' friends.

Successful men are also those who have been brought up with the women and are their neighbors; are handsome, good-looking and devoted to sexual pleasures, even though with their own servants; lovers of the daughters of the woman's nurse; those recently married; those who enjoy picnics and pleasure parties; those celebrated for being strong, enterprising and brave; lovers who surpass the husbands in learning and good looks; those with good qualities, liberal and free in their ways, and whose dress, manner of living and style are magnificent.

Women who are easily seduced are those who stand at the doors of their houses, and stare and looking sideways at passers-by; idle women who sit conversing with neighboring young men; those whose husbands have taken another wife without any just cause; who hate their husbands or are hated by them, and who have not borne any children, have nobody to

> *When a man is endeavoring to seduce one woman, he should not attempt to seduce another at the same time. But after he has succeeded with the first, and enjoyed her for a considerable time, he can start making up to another woman.*

look after them, or keep them in check; those who are very fond of society, and apparently very affectionate with everyone.

Men keen to make conquests are attracted towards the wives of actors; young and desirable widows; inaffluent girls and women, and those overly fond of enjoyment; wives of men with many younger brothers; vain women; those who consider their husbands inferior to themselves in rank or abilities; those proud of their skills in the arts; women mentally disturbed by the folly of their husbands; married in their infancy to rich men and disliking them when they grow up; those who desire men with dispositions, talents, and wisdom suitable to their own tastes; women slighted by their husbands without any cause; not respected by other women of the same rank or beauty as themselves; those whose husbands travel frequently; jeweler's' wives; jealous, covetous, immoral, barren, lazy and voluptuous women.

There are also *shlokas* on the subject :

Desire, which springs from nature and which is increased by art, and from which all danger is taken away by wisdom, becomes firm and secure. A clever man, depending on his own ability, and observing carefully the meaningful signs and gestures of women, and removing the causes of their turning away from men, is generally successful with them.

A clever man, depending on his own ability, and observing carefully the meaningful signs and gestures of women is generally successful with them.

GETTING ACQUAINTED

परिचयकारण प्रकरण

Parichayakarana Prakarana

 ncient sages believed that girls are more easily seduced directly by the man himself than by employing female messengers, but that others' wives are more easily approached through female messengers. In Vatsyayana's view a man should always act himself in these matters, and only when this is impracticable or impossible, should female messengers be employed. The belief that women who act and talk boldly and freely are to be won by the man's personal efforts, and others are to be approached by female messengers, is a fallacy.

Opportunities for Meeting

When a man takes the initiative, he should

A man should always employ female messengers to assist him in seducing another man's wife. (Left) After a girl has become acquainted with the man, and manifested her love for him by outward signs and her body language, the man should make every effort to win her over. Here Krishna , the eternal lover hides in a tree to witness the bare charms of his beloved.

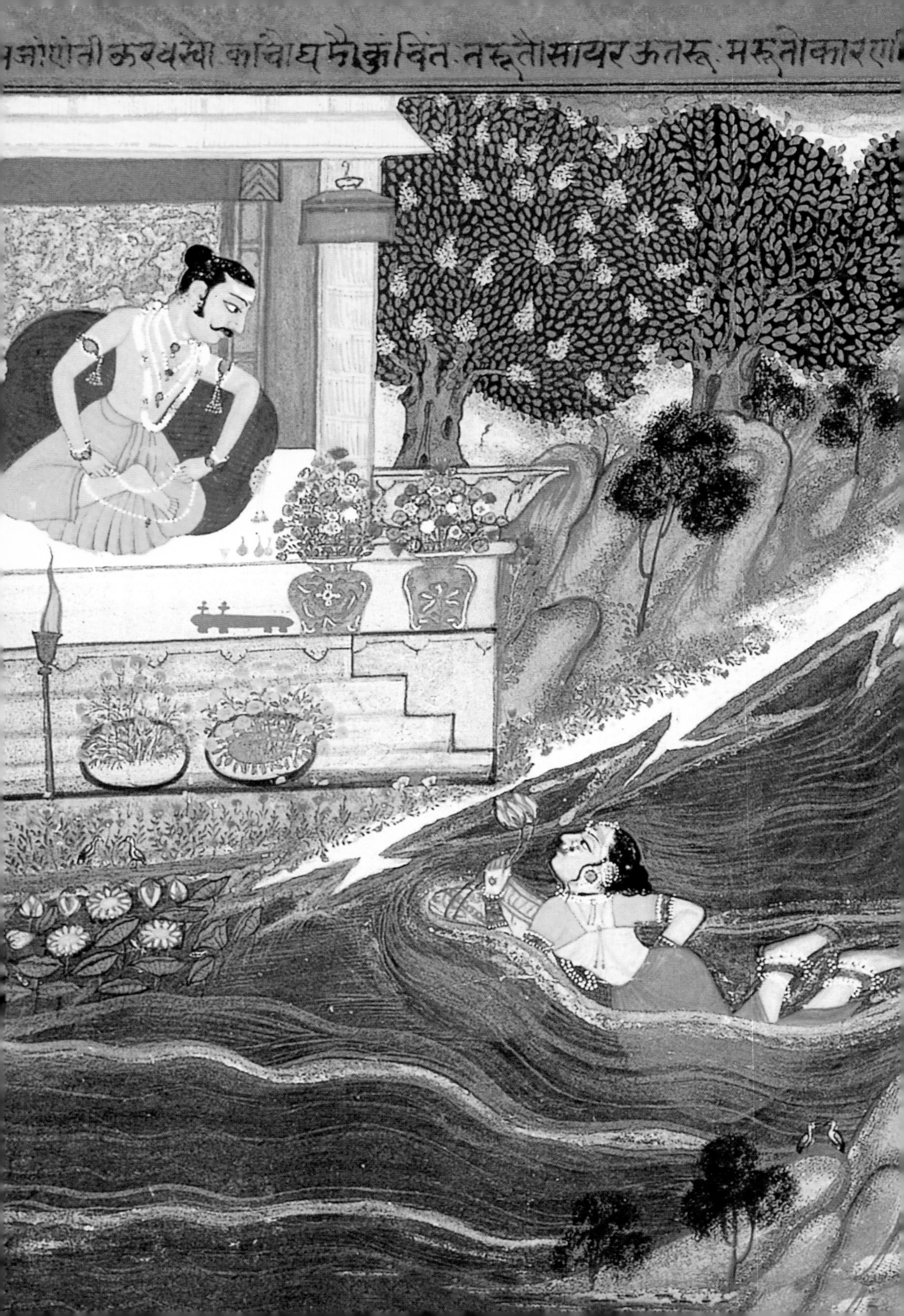

first make the acquaintance of the woman he loves, and arrange to be seen by her on a natural or special opportunity. A natural opportunity is when one of them goes to the other's house, and a special opportunity is when they meet at the house of a friend, caste-fellow, minister, or physician; or at marriage ceremonies, offerings, festivals, and garden parties.

When they do meet, he should be careful to indicate to her the state of his mind: he should pull his moustache, make a sound with his nails, make his ornaments tinkle, bite his lower lip, and do other similar things. When she looks at him he should speak to his friends about her and other women, and show her his liberality and his appreciation of enjoyment. When sitting with a female friend he should yawn and twist his body, contract his eyebrows, speak slowly as if weary, and listen with indifference. He should manifest his love by conducting a double-edged conversation with a child or some other person, apparently referring to a third person, but directed at the woman he loves. He should make signs with his nails or with a stick that have reference to her on the ground, and should embrace and kiss a young boy in her presence, give him a mixture of betel nut and betel leaves with his tongue, press his chin with his fingers, and fondle and caress other parts of the boy's body. All these actions should be covertly directed towards the woman.

The man should fondle the boy seated in her lap, give him something to play with, and then take the same back. He should converse with her about the boy, thus gradually becoming well acquainted with her, and make himself agreeable to her relations. Subsequently this acquaintanceship should be made a pretext for visiting her house frequently, and on such occasions he should converse on the subject of love in her absence but within her hearing. As his intimacy with her increases he should give her some

(Left) If she meets him once, and comes again to meet him better dressed that before, or comes to him in some lonely place, he can be certain that she is capable of being enjoyed with the use of a little force.

kind of deposit or trust, and take away from it a small portion at a time; or he may give her some fragrant substances, or betel nuts to be kept for him by her. After this he should endeavor to make her well acquainted with his own wife, and persuade them to carry on confidential conversations, and sit together in lonely places. In order to see her frequently he should arrange that both families employ the same goldsmith, jeweler, basket-maker, dyer, and washerman. He should pay her long visits openly under the pretense of conducting some business, and one business can lead to another, to keep up the intercourse between them. Whenever she wants anything, he should indicate his willingness and ability to give her money if she needs, or teach her an art that she wishes to acquire skill in - all these being within his power. In the company of other people, he should discuss the doings and sayings of other

persons, or show her jewellery and precious stones, the value of which she may be aware of, and if she disputes with him about the articles or their value, he should agree with her in every way.

Gifts and Presents

After a girl has become acquainted with the man, and manifested her love for him by outward signs and her body language, the man should make every effort to win her over. But as most girls are not acquainted with sexual union, they should be treated with delicacy, and the man should proceed with considerable caution, though in the case of women accustomed to sexual intercourse, this is not necessary. When the girl's intentions are known, and her bashfulness put aside, the man should begin to interchange clothes, rings, and flowers with her, taking care that the things given by him are handsome and valuable. He should receive from her a mixture of betel nut and betel leaves, and when going to a party, should ask for the flower in her hair or in her hand. If he gives her a flower, it should be a fragrant one, with marks made by his nails or teeth. With increasing assiduity he should dispel her fears, and gradually persuade her to go with him to a lonely place, and embrace and kiss her there. And finally when he gives her some betel nut, or receives the same from her, or exchanges flowers, he should touch and press her private parts, arouse her physically, and bring his efforts to a satisfactory climax.

One at a Time

When a man is endeavoring to seduce one woman, he should not attempt to seduce another at the same time. But after he has succeeded with the first, and enjoyed her for a considerable time, he can keep her affections by giving her presents, and then start making up to another woman. When he sees the woman's husband going to a place near his house, he should not enjoy the woman then, even though she may be easily won over at that time. A wise man who regards his reputation should not think of seducing a woman who is apprehensive, timid, not to be trusted, well guarded, or with vigilant in-laws.

While the gopis bathe nude in the river mischievous Krishna has run away with their clothes and has climbed a tree. When on pleading, requesting and appealing he doesn't give them back they are forced to forget their shame and modesty and unabashedly they climb the tree in their pursuit. (Left) A desperate young sadhu, holy man cannot stop himself from playing with the charms of an available seductress.

ASCERTAINING EMOTIONS

भावपरिक्षा प्रकरण

Bhavapariksha Prakarana

When a man is trying to gain over a woman he should examine the state of her mind, and test her behavior; if she listens to him, but does not manifest her own intentions, he should then try to win her over by means of a go-between.

Winning over the Woman

If she meets him once, and comes again to meet him better dressed that before, or comes to him in some lonely place, he can be certain that she is capable of being enjoyed with the use of a little force. A woman who lets a man make up to her, but does not give herself up even after a long time, should be considered as a trifler in love, but owing to the fickleness of the human mind, even such a woman can be conquered by always keeping up a close acquaintanceship with her.

When a woman ignores the man's attentions, and will not meet him or approach him out of respect for him and pride in herself,

---

(Left) With increasing desire he should dispel her fears, and gradually persuade her to go with him to a lonely place, and embrace and kiss her there. And finally he should touch and press her private parts, arouse her physically, and bring his efforts to a satisfactory climax.

she can be won over but with difficulty, either by keeping on familiar terms with her, or through a clever mediator.

A woman who reproaches the man with harsh words should be abandoned at once, but a woman who reproaches him affectionately, should be made love to in every way.

A woman who meets a man in a secluded place, and bears the touch of his foot, but pretends to ignore it because of her indecision, should be conquered by patience, and by continued effort. If she happens to go to sleep near him he should put his left arm around her, and when she awakens, judge whether she repulses him in reality, or only pretends to but actually desires it again. And what is done by the arm can also be done by the foot. If the man succeeds in this he should embrace her more closely, and if she gets

The inverted position allows the man to help himself to a smacking blow to his lover's alluring bottoms. (Left) If a woman desired by the king is living with a man who is not her husband, the king should have her arrested, make her a slave on account of her crime, should place her in custody. Or he should make his ambassador quarrel with the woman's husband, imprison her as the wife of his enemy, and by this means, place her in the royal inner court.

up and goes away, but behaves with him as usual the next day, he should consider her not unwilling. If, however, she does not come again, the man should try to win her over by means of a go-between; and if, after having disappeared for some time, she comes again, and behaves as usual, the man should then consider that she would not object to be united with him.

A Willing Woman

When a woman gives a man an opportunity, and manifests her own love, he should proceed to enjoy her. And she would make this evident by certain signs: she would call out to him without being addressed by him; she would expose the erogenous parts of her body in secret places, when the opportunity occurs; she would speaks to him tremblingly and inarticulately, her face glistening with beads of perspiration; she would massage his body and press his head; when massaging she would use one hand only, and with the other, touch and embrace the secret parts of his body.

At times she would place both hands and remain still as if she has been surprised by something, or overcome by fatigue. She would also sometimes bend her face down upon his thighs, and when asked to press and fondle them, would not be unwilling to do so. After placing one of her hands motionless on his body, she would not remove it even though the man would press it between the two members of his body. Lastly,

The go-between should talk to the woman about the weakness of her husband's passion, his jealousy, roguery, ingratitude, aversion to enjoyments, dullness, meanness, and all his other faults that she may know of. (Left) He should visit her house frequently under the pretense of conducting some business, and on such occasions he should converse on the subject of love. One business can lead to another, to keep up the intercourse between them.

when she has resisted all the efforts of the man to win her over, she would return to him the next day to massage his body again. When a woman neither encourages a man, nor avoids him, but isolates herself, she must be approached through her female servant. If when called by the man, she acts in the same way, then a skillful go-between can be tried. But if she has nothing to say to the man, he should reconsider well before trying to win her over. Some *shlokas* on the subject state:

A man should first get himself introduced to a woman, and then carry on a conversation with her. He should give her hints of his love for her, and if he finds from her replies that she receives these hints favorably, he should then set to work to gain her over without any fear. A woman who shows her love by outward signs to the man at his first meeting should be gained over very easily. In the same way a lascivious woman, who when addressed in loving words replies openly in words expressive of her love, should be considered to have been gained over at that very moment. With regard to all women, whether they be wise, simple, or confiding, this rule is laid down that those who make an open manifestation of their love are easily gained over.

The impatient man seizes the opportunity and sneaks onto the wife from behind who uninterruptedly continues to pound spices.

DUTIES OF A GO-BETWEEN

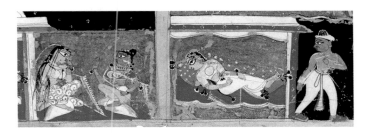

दूतीकर्म प्रकरण

Dootikarma Prakarana

I f a woman has manifested her love or desire either by signs or by her body language, and is afterwards rarely or never seen anywhere, or if a woman is met for the first time, the man should get a clever friend to approach her.

Behavior of a Go-between

The friend, having wheedled herself into the woman's confidence, should try to make her despise her husband by her artful conversation, tell her about medicines for begetting children, talk to her about other people, recite tales of various kinds and stories about other men's wives; praise her beauty, wisdom, generosity and good nature, and then say to her: "It is indeed a pity that you, who are so excellent a woman in every way, should be possessed of a husband of this kind. Beautiful lady, he is not fit even to serve you". The go-between should also talk to the woman about the weakness of her husband's passion, his jealousy, roguery, ingratitude, aversion to enjoyment, dullness, meanness, and all his other faults that she may know of. She should particularly stress that fault or failing by which the wife appears to be the

most affected. If the wife is a deer woman, and the husband a hare man, then there would be no fault; but if he is a hare man, and she a mare or elephant woman, then this fault should be pointed out to her.

Gonikaputra believes that when it is the woman's first affair, or when her love has only been very secretly shown, the man should send a go-between with whom she may already be acquainted, and in whom she confides.

The go-between should tell the woman about the man's obedience and love, and as her confidence and affection increase, she should explain her mission to her thus: "Hear this, O beautiful lady, that this man, born of a good family, having seen you, has gone mad on your account. The poor young man has a tender nature, and is in such distress that it is highly probable that he will succumb to his present affliction, and experience the pains of death". If the woman listens with a favorable ear, and the go-between observes her good spirit in her face, eyes, and conversation, then on the following day she should again bring up the subject of the man, and tell her the stories of Ahalya and Indra, Shakuntala and Dushyanta, and other such appropriate tales. She should also describe to her the man's strength, his talents,

Taken over by desire, cowgirls swirl and swoon around Krishna. (Left) When the woman manifests her love, the go-between should increase it by bringing her love tokens from the man, by extolling his good qualities, and telling her stories about his love for her.

his skill in the sixty-four arts mentioned by Babhravya, his good looks, and his liaison with some praiseworthy woman, even though this may not be true.

Behavior of the Woman with the Go-between

In addition, the go-between should carefully note the behavior of the woman. If it is favorable, she should address her with a smiling look, seat herself close beside her and ask, "Where have you been? What have you been doing? Where did you dine? Where did you sleep? Where have you been sitting?" The woman too should meet the go-between in secluded places and tell her stories there, yawn contemplatively, draw long sighs, give her presents, remember her on festivals, dismiss her with a wish to see her again, and say to her jestingly, "Oh, well-speaking woman, why do you speak these bad words to me?" She should discourse on the sin of her union with the man, not tell her about any previous visits or conversations with him, but wish to be asked about them, and lastly, should laugh at the man's desire, but not reproach him in any way.

Carrying Love Tokens

When the woman manifests her love in the manner described above, the go-between should increase it by bringing her love tokens from the man. But if the woman is not personally acquainted with the man, the go-between should win her over by extolling his good qualities, and telling her stories about his love for her. Auddalaka says that when a man and woman are not acquainted with each other, and have not shown each other any signs of affection, the employment of a go-between is not of much use. Babhravya, on the other hand, affirms that even though they are personally unacquainted, but have shown each other signs of affection, there is an occasion for the employment of a go-between. Gonikaputra asserts that a go-between should be employed if they are acquainted, even though no signs of affection may have passed between them. Vatsyayana maintains that even though they are not personally acquainted, and may not have shown each other any signs of affection, still they are both capable of placing confidence in a go-between.

The go-between should show the woman the betel nut and betel leaves, the perfumes, flowers, rings and other presents which the man may have given for her, and on which should be impressed the marks of the man's teeth and nails, and other signs. On the cloth that he sends he should illustrate with saffron both his hands joined together as if in earnest entreaty.

A go-between can raise enmity between any two lovers if she wishes to do so, or extol the loveliness of any woman that she wishes to praise. She can also speak highly of a man's skill in sexual enjoyment, and of the desire of other women, more beautiful even than the woman he is addressing. (Left) If the husband is a hare man, and the wife a mare or elephant woman, then this fault should be pointed out to her by the go-between sent by the willing lover.

The go-between should also show the woman ornamental figures of various kinds cut in leaves, ear ornaments, and chaplet made of flowers containing love letters expressing the man's desire, and persuade her to send affectionate presents to the man in return. After they have mutually accepted each other's presents, then a meeting should be arranged between them on the faith of the go-between.

Suitable Meeting Places

The followers of Babhravya say that this meeting should take place at the temple, or at fairs, garden parties, theatrical performances, marriages, sacrifices, festivals, when going to the river to bathe, or at times of natural calamities, fear of robbers or hostile invasions. Gonikaputra is of the opinion, however, that these meetings are better arranged in the abodes of female friends, mendicants, astrologers, and ascetics. But Vatsyayana asserts that the only place well suited for the purpose is one which has proper means of ingress and egress, and where arrangements have been made to prevent any accidental occurrence, and when a man who has once entered the house can also leave it without any disagreeable encounter.

Different Kinds of Female Messengers

The go-betweens or female messengers are of the following kinds: A woman who, having observed the mutual passion of a man and woman, and brings them together with the power of her own intellect, is called a go-between who takes upon herself the whole burden. This kind of go-between is chiefly employed when the man and the woman are already acquainted with each other, and have conversed together, and in such cases she is sent not only by the man, as is always done in all other cases, but by the woman too. This name is also given to a go-between who, perceiving that the man and the woman are suited to each other, tries to bring

---

(Left) Women of cities and towns generally visit the apartments of the royal ladies, as they are acquainted with them, and spend the night in conversation, sports and amusements. On such occasions a female attendant of the king, previously acquainted with the woman whom the king desires, should loiter about, and accost her when she sets out to go home, and lead her to the king.

about a union between them, even though they are not acquainted with each other.

A person who, perceiving that the affair has already begun, or that the man has already made advances, and completes the rest of the business, is called a go-between with limited powers.

A go-between who simply carries messages between a man and a woman, who love each other, but who cannot frequently meet, is said to be a letter bearer. This name is also given to one who is sent by either of the lovers to acquaint the other with the time and place of their meeting.

A woman who goes herself to a man, and tells him of her having enjoyed sexual union with him in a dream, expresses her anger at his wife having rebuked him for calling her by the name of her rival, gives him a token with the marks of her teeth and nails, informs him that she knew she was formerly desired by him, and asks him privately whether she or his wife is better looking, is a go-between for herself. Such a woman should be met and interviewed by the man privately and secretly.

This name is also given to a woman who, agreeing to act as a go-between for some other woman, wins over the man to herself, and thus causes the other woman to fail. The same applies to a man who, acting as a go-between for another, and having no previous connection with the woman, wins her for himself, thus causing the failure of the other man.

A woman who gains the confidence of an innocent young wife, learns her secrets without coercion, finds out about her husband's behavior, and then teaches her the art of securing his favor by adorning herself to show her love, instructing her how and when to be angry, or pretending to be so, and then, having herself made marks of the nails and teeth on the wife's body, gets her to send for her husband to show these marks to him and excite him, is known as **the go-between of an innocent young woman.** In such cases the man should send replies to his wife through the same woman.

When a man gets his wife to gain the confidence of a woman whom he wants to enjoy, and to call on her and talk to her about his wisdom and ability, she is termed **a wife serving as a go-between.** In this case the feelings of the woman with regard to the man should also be made known through the wife.

If a man sends a girl or a female servant to a woman under some pretext, and places a letter in her bouquet of flowers, or in her ear ornaments, or marks something about her with his teeth or nails, that messenger is called **a mute go-between.** In this case the man should expect an answer from the woman through her.

A person who carries a message with a double meaning, to a woman, or one which relates to some past transactions, or is unintelligible to other people, is said to be **a go-between adept in the art of secret codes.** In this case the reply

The nayaka enters the palace disguising himself as a guard and engages his beloved who is one of the women of the king's harem. Even though he knows the secret entrance to the harem, he should enter only if he safely knows his way out. (Left) By folding her legs upwards the nayika allows her lover an entry from below.

should be obtained through the same person.

There are some *shlokas* on the subject:

A female astrologer, servant, beggar, and a female artist are well acquainted with the business of a go-between, and very soon gain the confidence of other women. Any one of them can raise enmity between any two persons if she wishes to do so, or extol the loveliness of any woman that she wishes to praise, or describe the arts practiced by other women in sexual union. They can also speak highly of the love of a man, or his skill in sexual enjoyment, and of the desire of other women, more beautiful even than the woman they are addressing, for him, and explain the restraint under which he may be at home.

Lastly a go-between can, by the artfulness of her conversation, unite a woman with a man, even though he may not have been thought of by her, or may have been considered beyond her aspirations. She can also bring back a man to a woman, who, owing to some cause or other, has separated himself from her.

The nayika *swings in her lover's arms as he plays with both her nipples.*

Behavior of a king

ईश्वरकामित प्रकरण

Ishwarkamita Prakarana

ings and their ministers have no access to the abodes of others, and their mode of living is constantly watched, observed and imitated by their people, just as the animal world follows the sun - getting up at sunrise, and retiring when the sun sets in the evening. Persons in authority, therefore, should not commit any improper act in public, as this would be deserving of censure. But if they find that such an act is absolutely necessary, they should use the proper means as described here.

Seduction by Men of Lower Ranks

The headman of the village, the king's officer employed there, and the gleaner of corn, can gain over female villagers simply by asking them, and these women are called unchaste women by voluptuaries. There are several opportunities for these men to unite with these kind of women on occasions such as payment to labor; filling the granaries in their houses; cleaning the houses and taking things in and out; working in the fields; purchasing cotton, wool, flax,

hemp, and thread at appropriate seasons; selling and exchanging various other articles, and performing other tasks. Similarly the superintendents of cow pens enjoy the women working there; and the officers, who have the superintendence of widows, women without supporters, and women who have left their husbands, have sexual intercourse with these women. The city officer, while on his night rounds, takes advantage of his position and is able to enjoy lone women by virtue of his familiarity with their secrets. The superintendents of markets too have a great deal to do with the female villagers when the latter make purchases in the market.

Luring Women to the Palace

During the festival of the eighth moon, during the bright half of the month of *Margashirsha*, as also during the moonlight festival of the month of *Kartika*, and the spring festival of *Chaitra*, the women of cities and towns generally visit the women of the king's court in the king's palace. These visitors go to the several apartments of the royal ladies, as they are acquainted with them, and spend the night in conversation, sports and amusements, and go home in the morning. On such occasions a female attendant of the king, previously acquainted with the woman whom the king desires, should loiter about, and accost her when she sets out to go home, and induce her to come back to the palace. Prior to these festivals, she should have intimated to the woman that on this occasion she would show her all the interesting things in the royal palace. Accordingly she should show her the bower in the garden house with its floor inlaid with marble, the bower of grapes, the pavilion in the water, the secret passages, paintings, sporting animals, birds, and cages of lions and tigers. After this, when alone with her, with a strict promise of secrecy, she should tell her about

(Pages 222-223) The king delights in sexual union in the sitting position with one of the women of his harem. The couple's desire for each other is evident from the way he smothers her breasts with both hands and the way she hold his lingam for a guided entry. (Left) Radha and Krishna in cosy dalliance amidst a profusion of lotus blossoms.

the king's love for her, and the good fortune that would come her way upon her union with the king. If the woman does not accept the offer, she should conciliate and please her with handsome presents befitting the position of the king, and having accompanied her for a distance, should dismiss her with great affection.

Having become acquainted with the husband of the woman the king desires, the king's wives should get the woman to visit them in the inner court; on this occasion a female attendant of the king, should be sent and instructed to act suitably.

One of the king's wives should send a female attendant to the woman the king desires. She, in turn, should become intimate with her, and persuade her to come to the royal abode.

Role of the King's Wife

The king's wife should invite the woman the king desires, to come to the royal palace, to observe her practice the art in which she, herself, may be skilled and thus be influenced to accede to the king's desires.

A woman desired by the king, and whose husband may have lost his wealth, or may have some cause to fear the king, should be taken aside by a female mendicant in league with the king's wife,

The energetic young couple get entangled during a stormy and explosive union.
(Left) I shall arrange for your entrance into the palace, and you will have no cause to fear any danger from the king. If the woman accepts this offer, the female mendicant should take her a few times to the inner court, and the king's wife should promise her protection. When the woman, delighted with her reception, visits the inner court again, she is taken advantage of by the king.

and told: "The king's wife has influence over him, and and is naturally kind-hearted; we must therefore go to her for help. I shall arrange for your entrance into the palace, and you will have no cause to fear any danger from the king". If the woman accepts this offer, the female mendicant should take her a few times to the inner court, and the king's wife should promise her protection. When the woman, delighted with her reception, visits the inner court again, she is taken advantage of by the king.

This strategy also applies to the wives of those who seek service under the king, those oppressed by the king's ministers, those who are poor, not satisfied with their position, who desire to gain the king's favor, who wish to become famous among the people, who are oppressed by members of their own caste, who want to injure their caste-fellows, who are spies of the king, or who have any other object to attain.

The Powers of the King

If a woman desired by the king is living with a man who is not her husband, the king should have her arrested, make her a slave on account of her crime, should place her in custody. Or he should make his ambassador quarrel with the woman's husband, imprison her as the wife of his enemy, and by this means, place her in the royal inner court.

These ways of winning over other men's wives are mainly practiced in kings' palaces. But a king should never enter another's abode, for Abhira, the king of the Kottas, was killed by a washerman while in the house of another, and similarly, Jayasena, the king of the Kashis, was slain by the commander of his cavalry.

But according to the customs of some countries there are facilities for kings to make love to the wives of other men. In Andhra, newly married daughters of the people enter the king's palace with gifts on the tenth day of their marriage, and after having been enjoyed by the king, are then dismissed. In the region of the Vatsagulmas the wives of the chief ministers approach the king at night to serve him. In Vidarbha the beautiful wives of the inhabitants pass a month in the king's court under the pretense of affection for the king. In the region of the Aparantakas the people give their beautiful wives as presents to the ministers and kings. And in Saurashtra, the women of the city and the villages enter the inner court for the king's pleasure.

There are also two *shlokas* on the subject :

The above and other ways are the means employed in different countries by kings with regard to the wives of other persons. But a king, who has the welfare of his people at heart, should not on any account put them into practice. A king who has conquered the six enemies of mankind: lust, anger, avarice, spiritual ignorance, pride and envy, becomes the master of the whole earth.

While going to the river to bathe is an ideal opportunity for a young nayika *to skip away from the group to meet her waiting lover.*

Conduct of the ladies of the inner court

अन्तःपुरिकावृत्त प्रकरण

Antahpurikavritta Prakarana

The women of the royal house are strictly guarded, and cannot see or meet any other men or have their desires satisfied, their husband being common to all of them. Hence they give pleasure to each other in various ways.

Achieving Pleasure in Various Ways

Having dressed the daughters of their nurses, female friends or attendants like men, they accomplish their object by means of bulbs, roots, and fruits shaped like the *lingam*, or they lie down upon the statue of a male figure, in which the *lingam* is visible and erect.

Some kings who are compassionate, take or apply certain medicines to be able to enjoy many wives in one night, simply to satisfy the desires of their wives, even though they perhaps have no desire of their own. Others enjoy only those wives they particularly

---

(Left) An anxious nayika of the king's harem has secretly smuggled in her lover with the help of her attendant and derives the pleasures of sexual union by donning the male role.

like, while others take them according to turns. These practices are prevalent in Eastern countries, and different means of enjoyment used by females are also taken recourse to by males.

Some men who are unable to obtain a woman, satisfy their desires by unnatural intercourse with animals like a mare, a she-goat, a bitch; or with an artificial *yoni* or figure of a woman; and by masturbation.

Clandestine Entry by Men into the Inner Court

The ladies of the royal court use their female attendants to get men disguised as women into their apartments. Those attendants who are acquainted with their secrets, and daughters of their nurses, who are acquainted with their secrets, lure men into the inner court by telling them of their good fortune, describing the ease of entering and departure, the large size of the premises, and the carelessness of the sentinels. But these women should never induce a man to enter the palace by telling him falsehoods, for that may lead to his destruction.

The man himself should be aware of the numerous disasters he may have to face when he enters a royal house, even though it may be easily accessible. He should ascertain that there is an easy way out, check if it is closely surrounded by pleasure gardens, if it has separate enclosures, if the sentinels are careless, and if the king has gone abroad. Then, when he is called by the women of the court, he should very carefully observe the locality, and enter by the way picked out by them.

The nayika *widens her legs apart to accommodate her lover's huge* lingam. *(Pagesw 232-233) Krishna with* gopis. *(Left) Some kings who are compassionate, take or apply certain medicines to be able to enjoy many wives in one night. Others enjoy only those wives they particularly like, while others take them according to turns. Here the king and his beloved adopt a rather impossible posture.*

If he can, he should hang around the palace every day, make friends with the sentinels, and show his closeness to the court's female attendants, who may know of his design, and express his regret to them at not being able to obtain the object of his desire. He should leave it to them to arrange a go-between, who has access to the inner court, and he should be careful about recognizing the king's emissaries.

If the go-between has no access to the court, he should stand in a place where the lady he loves and whom he is anxious to enjoy, can be seen. If that place is occupied by the king's sentinels, he should go there disguised as a female attendant of a lady who visits the place. When she looks at him he should let her know his feelings by signs and gestures, show her pictures, things with double meanings, chaplet of flowers, and rings. He should take careful note of her response by word or sign or gesture, and then try and get into the palace. If he is certain of her coming to a particular

A royal couple embraces and enjoys the dancer's performance. (Left) This fancy and acrobatic posture was probably devised by the artist to amuse the king and praise his abilities both in the fields of hunting and lovemaking.

place, he should conceal himself there, and at the appointed time, enter with her as one of the guards. He may also go in and out, concealed in a folded bed, or bed covering, or with his body made invisible by means of external applications. A recipe for one of these is: to burn the heart of *nakula*, an inchneumont, the fruit of the *tumbi*, long gourd, and the eyes of a serpent without letting out smoke. The ashes are then ground and mixed with water in equal quantities and by putting this on the eyes a man may go about unseen. Other means of invisibility are prescribed by Duyana Brahmans and tantrics.

Again he may enter the inner court during the festival of the eighth moon in the month of Margashirsha, and during the moonlight festivals when the female attendants are all busy or distracted.

The following principles are laid down: the entrance and exit of young men into palaces generally take place when things are being brought in and out of the palace, during drinking festivals when the female attendants are in a hurry, when the residence of some royal ladies is being changed, when the king's wives go to gardens, or to fairs, and enter the palace on their return, or lastly, when the king is away on a long pilgrimage. The women of the royal palace know each other's secrets, and having a common object, they assist each other. A young man who enjoys all of them, and who is common to them all, can continue enjoying his union with them so long as it is kept a secret.

Varying Customs and Practices in Royal Courts

In the region of the Aparantakas the royal

The ladies of the royal court use their female attendants to get men disguised as women into their apartments. Here a man with a fancy hairdo engages the nayika in a difficult upside down posture. (Left) Lovers adopt a rhythmic and sporty approach to their love play with their elegant dance like movements.

ladies are not well protected, and many young men are brought into the court by women who have access to the royal palace. The wives of the king of Ahira accomplish their object with the palace sentinels who bear the name of Kshatriyas. The royal ladies in the region of Vatsagulmas arrange for suitable men to enter the palace with their female messengers. In Vidharba, the royal sons enter when they please, and enjoy the women, with the exception of their own mothers. In Stri Rajya the queens are enjoyed by their caste-fellows and relations. In Gauda, the royal wives are enjoyed by Brahmins, friends, servants and slaves, and in Sindhudesh, by servants, foster children, and other such persons. In Himavata, adventurous citizens bribe the sentinels and enter the court. In the region of the Vanyas and the Kamyas, Brahmans, with the king's knowledge, enter the court to give flowers to the ladies, converse with them from behind a curtain, and enjoy sexual union. The women in the private apartments of the king of the Prachyas conceal a vigorous young man for every group of nine or ten of them.

Protecting One's Wife

Ancient sages say a king should select men whose freedom from carnal desires is well tested, as palace sentinels. But such men, through fear or avarice, may allow other persons to enter. Therefore, Gonikaputra states that kings should place such men whose freedom from fears and avarice also has been well tested. Vatsyayana affirms that people might be admitted under the influence of *dharma*, and therefore the men selected should not only be free from carnal desires, fear and avarice, but also be unquestionably loyal.

The followers of Brabhravya assert that a man should make his wife associate with a young woman who would tell him others' secrets and about his wife's chastity. But Vatsyayana maintains that since wicked persons are always successful with women, a man should not let his innocent wife be corrupted by the company of a deceitful woman.

The contributing causes of the loss of a woman's chastity are: going to social gatherings; absence of restraint and caution in her relations with other men; continued and long absence of her husband; living in a foreign country; the company of loose women; neglect of her love and feelings by her husband and vying with him.

Some *shlokas* state:

A clever man, learning from the Shastras *the ways of winning over the wives of other people, is never deceived in the case of his own wives. No one, however, should make use of these ways for seducing the wives of others, because they do not always succeed, and, moreover, often cause disasters, and the destruction of* dharma *and* artha. *This book which is intended for the good of the people, and to teach them the ways of guarding their own wives, should not be made use of merely for gaining over the wives of others.*

A prince and his royal ladies in a pleasure palace.

The Courtesan

Beguiling the right man

Living as his wife

Acquiring wealth

Reconciliation

Special gains

Gains and losses

BOOK 6

Beguiling the right man

सहायगम्यागम्यगमनकारणचिन्ताप्रकरण

Sahayagamyagamyagamanakaranachinta Prakarana

This book about courtesans was compiled by Vatsyayana from a treatise on the subject written by Dattaka for the women of Pataliputra, Patna, some two thousand years ago. Dattaka's work is not extant now, but this abridgement of it is very useful.

Although a great deal has been written on the subject, there is no better description of the courtesan, her belongings, her ideas, and the working of her mind.

The Courtesan in Ancient India

The domestic and social life of the early Hindus would not be complete without mention of the courtesan who was recognized as a part of society, and so long as she behaved with decency and propriety, she was regarded with a certain respect. She was never treated in the East with that brutality and contempt common in the West, and her education was always superior to the rest of womankind in Asia.

In earlier days the well-educated Hindu dancing girl and courtesan

(Left) The artist is ever ready to put his brush to portray the many facets of love, as this miniature from Rajasthan depicts.

doubtless resembled the Hetera of the Greeks, and was far more acceptable as a companion than the married or unmarried women of that period. At all times there has been a little rivalry between the chaste and the unchaste. But while some women are born courtesans and follow the instincts of their nature in every class of society, it has been truly said by some authors that every woman is instinctively coquettish, and does her best, as a general rule, to make herself agreeable to the male sex.

By having intercourse with men, courtesans obtain sexual pleasure as well as their own maintenance. When a courtesan takes up with a man for love, the action is natural; but when she resorts to him for money, her action is artificial or forced. But even then, she should conduct herself as if her love is indeed natural, because men repose confidence in women who love them. In showing her love to the man, she should also display freedom from avarice, and for the sake of her future credit, abstain from acquiring money from him by unlawful means.

Desirable Patrons and Protectors

A courtesan, well dressed and wearing ornaments, should sit or stand at the door of her house to be seen by passers-by on the public road, since she is like an object on view for sale. She should form friendships with those persons who would enable her to lure men away from other women, and attach them to herself; to repair her own misfortunes; to acquire wealth, and to protect herself from being bullied by persons with whom she may have dealings. These persons would include: the guard of the town, or the police; officers of the courts of justice; astrologers; powerful or learned men; men with vested interests; teachers of the sixty-four arts; *pithamardas*, *vitas*, *vidushakas*, flower-sellers, perfumers, vendors of spirits, washermen, barbers, beggars, and any others who may be necessary in her line of work.

(Left) This 20th century pata, painting on cloth, from Orissa, shows the woman's legs in a wide, yawning position, while she is supported on her lover's lap.

The men to be taken up with for the purpose of getting their money, are:

men of independent income; young, handsome men, men free of ties; those who hold positions of authority under the king; who have secured their means of livelihood; who possess unfailing sources of income and are full of self-praise; who have feminine traits, but wish to be thought of as men; who hate their equals; who are naturally liberal; who have influence with the king or his ministers; who disobey their elders and are kept an eye on by their caste-members; only sons of wealthy fathers; ascetics internally troubled with desire; brave men; physicians of the king and previous acquaintances.

Qualities of a *Nayaka*, hero, and a *Nayika*, Heroine

Those who possess excellent qualities should be resorted to for the sake of love, and fame. Such men are of high birth and learning, eloquent and energetic, worldly-wise with orderly habits, poets, storytellers, skilled in various art, far-sighted with great minds, full of perseverance, firm devotion, free from disease with perfect bodies, strong, not addicted to drinking, sexually powerful, sociable, attractive, show love towards women but are not entirely devoted to them, who have an independent means of livelihood, and are free from envy and suspicion.

The woman should also have the following characteristics: beauty,

---

By having intercourse with men, courtesans obtain sexual pleasure as well a their own maintenance. Even when she takes up a man only for money she should conduct herself in such a way as if her love is indeed natural. (Right) A courtesan must not resort to a man who is sick or has foul breath.

amiability, auspicious body marks, a firm mind, appreciation of others' good qualities, a desire for wealth; delight in sexual union resulting from love, and the same class as the man with regard to sexual enjoyment. She should be anxious to acquire experience and knowledge, be free from avarice, and enjoy social gatherings and the arts.

The natural qualities of all women: intelligence, a cheerful disposition, good manners; straightforwardness in behavior, gratefulness; foresight; consistency, orderly habits; absence of meanness, malignity, anger, avarice, dullness and stupidity; knowledge of the *Kama Shastras,* and skill in all the arts.

The following men are not to be resorted to by courtesans: a man who is consumptive, sickly, affected by hook worms, with bad breath; whose wife is dear to him; who speaks harshly, is suspicious, avaricious, pitiless, extremely bashful, conceited; a thief; one who likes sorcery; is indifferent to respect or disrespect; can be won over even by his enemies by money.

Why Prostitutes Accept Lovers

Ancient sages opined that a courtesan resorted to men due to love, fear, money, pleasure, revenge, curiosity, sorrow, need for constant intercourse, duty, being a celebrity, compassion, friendship, shame, similarity to a beloved person, avoiding the love of somebody else, being of the same class as the man with respect to sexual union, living in the same place, constancy, and poverty. But Vatsyayana asserts that desire of wealth, freedom from misfortune, and love are the only causes that affect the union of courtesans with men.

A courtesan should not sacrifice money for love, because money is the chief objective. But if afraid, she should pay regard to strength and other qualities. Even though she is invited by a man to join him, she should not consent at once, because men despise what is easily acquired. On such occasions she should first send her masseurs, singers, and jesters, or in their absence, the *pithamardas*, confidants, and others to ascertain his feelings and state of mind, and gauge whether he is pure or impure, affected or the reverse, capable of attachment or indifferent, liberal or niggardly. If then, she likes him, she should employ the *vita* and others to attract his attention.

Accordingly, the *pithamarda* should bring the man to her house, ostensibly to see the fights of quails, cocks, and rams; to hear the mynah talk, or see the practice of some art; or he may take the woman to the man's abode. After this, when the man comes to her house the woman should affectionately give him a present to excite his curiosity and love, telling him that it was specially designed for his use. She should amuse him with stories, and delight him with her actions. When he goes away she should frequently send him a small gift with a female attendant, who is skilled in carrying on a jesting conversation. Sometimes, accompanied by the *pithamarda*, she should go to him herself under the pretense of business.

Some *shlokas* on the subject state:

When a lover comes to her abode, a courtesan should give him a mixture of betel leaves and betel nut, garlands of flowers, and perfumed ointments, and showing her skill in arts, entertain him with a long

A man who is consumptive, has bad breath, who speaks harshly or is indifferent or disrespectful should not be resorted to by a courtesan.
(Left) A courtesan should be well versed in the sixty-four arts, specially the art of dancing and entertaining her admirers.

conversation. She should also give him some loving presents, and exchange her own things with his, and at the same time, show him her skill in sexual enjoyment. When a courtesan is thus united with her lover she should always delight him by affectionate gifts, conversation, and by the application of tender means of enjoyment.

LIVING AS HIS WIFE

कान्तावृत्तप्रकरण

Kantavritta Prakarana

When a courtesan lives as a wife with her lover, she should behave like a chaste woman, and do everything to his satisfaction. Her duty is to give him pleasure, but she should not become attached to him, even though pretending to be so.

To accomplish this, she should have a mother dependent on her - one who is harsh and looks upon money as her chief object in life. If she has no mother, then an old and confidential nurse should play the same role. The mother or nurse should show her displeasure to the lover, and forcibly take her away from him. The woman herself, accompanied by the *pithamarda*,

---

(Left) A courtesan should be beautiful, amiable, should have auspicious body marks, a firm mind, and a desire for wealth and should take delight in sexual union.

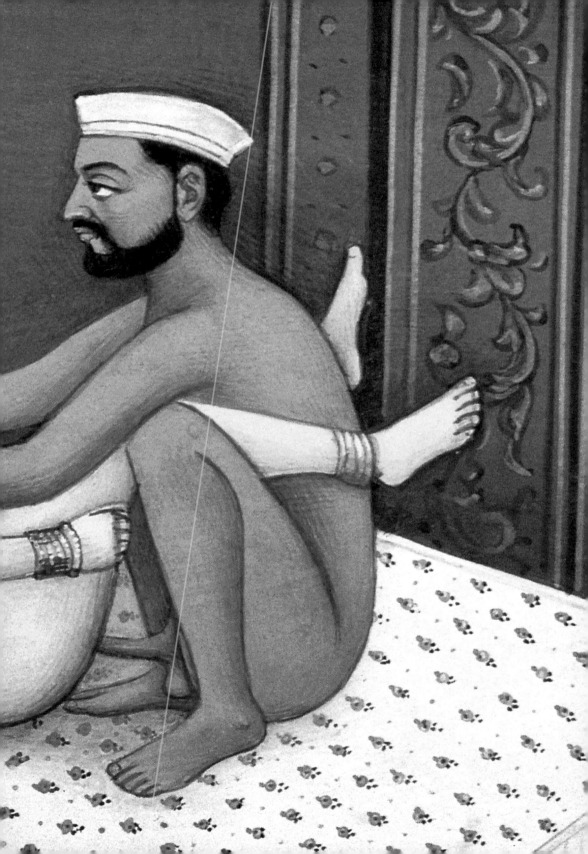

should always pretend anger, dejection, fear, and shame on this account, but should not disobey the mother or nurse at any time.

Gaining the Lover's Favor

She should tell her mother or nurse that the man is suffering from ill health, and use this pretext to visit him. She should also do the following to gain his favor: send her female attendant to bring the flowers used by him on the previous day, and use them herself as a mark of affection, as also the mixture of betel nut and leaves uneaten by him; express wonder at his knowledge of sexual intercourse, and the means of enjoyment used by him, learn from him the sixty-four kinds of pleasure described by Babhravya; continually practice the ways of enjoyment that he likes; keep his secrets; tell him her own desires and secrets; conceal her anger;

(Pages 254-255) When a courtesan lives as a wife with her lover, she should behave like a chaste woman, and do everything to his satisfaction. Her duty is to give him pleasure, but she should not become attached to him, even though pretending to be so. (Left and Below) The young man is completely besotted by his beautiful and skillful courtesan who by her display of love and her knowledge of the sixty four kinds of pleasures learned from the Kama Shastras *has totally won him over.*

never neglect him in bed when he turns towards her; touch him where he wishes; kiss and embrace him when he is asleep; look at him with apparent anxiety when he is lost in thought; show neither complete shamelessness, nor excessive bashfulness when he meets her, or sees her standing on the terrace of her house from the public road; hate his enemies; and love those who are dear to him. She should match his temperament and be in high or low spirits according to his mood; express curiosity to see his wives; contain her anger; evince suspicion that the marks and wounds on his body made by her own nails and teeth have been made by another woman; show her love for him through deeds, signs, and hints; remain silent when he is asleep, intoxicated, or sick; be attentive when he describes his good actions, and recite them afterwards to his praise and benefit; give him witty replies if he is sufficiently attached to her; listen to all his stories, except those that relate to her rivals; express dejection and sorrow if he sighs, yawns, or falls down; wish him a long life when he sneezes; pretend to be ill, or state a desire to be pregnant.

The courtesan should also abstain from praising anybody else, or censuring those with the same faults as him; abstain from wearing her ornaments, and eating when he is in pain, sick, low-spirited, or suffering from misfortune. Instead she should condole and lament with him; wish to accompany him if he is leaving the country or is banished from it by the king; express a desire not to live after him; telling him that the whole object and desire of her life is to be united with him; offer promised

The shy heroine hides her breasts using her long dark tresses. (Left) The woman supported by her lover's strong arms places herself in the position of suspended congress and skillfully thrusts forward to give him maximum pleasure.

sacrifices to the deity when he acquires wealth, or fulfills a desire, or recovers from an illness or disease; wear ornaments every day; act with circumspection; recite his name and that of his family in her songs; place his hand on her loins, bosom, and forehead, and fall asleep after feeling the pleasure of his touch; sit on his lap and fall asleep there.

Vows, fasts, and prayers

Dissuading him from vows and fasts, she should say, "Let the sin fall upon me", but keep the vows and fasts with him if it is impossible to change his mind. She should emphasize that they are difficult to observe, even by herself, if he has any dispute about them. Looking on her own wealth and his without any distinction, she ought to abstain from going to public assemblies without him, and accompany him when he does; take delight in using things previously used by him, and in eating food that he has left uneaten; venerate his family, his disposition, skill in the arts, his learning, his caste, complexion, birthplace, friends, good qualities, age, and sweet temper; ask him to sing, and perform other similar acts if he can; go to him without regard to fear, cold, heat, or rain; state that he should be her lover even in the next world; adapt her tastes, disposition and actions to his; abstain from sorcery; dispute continually with her mother about going to him, and if forcibly taken by her mother to some other place, express her desire to die by taking poison, starving, stabbing herself, or by hanging; assure the man of her constancy and love through her agents, and receive money herself, but abstain from any financial dispute with her mother.

When the man sets out on a journey, she should make him swear to return quickly, and in his absence observe her vows of worshipping the deity, and wear no ornaments except those that are

(Left) The two rishis in positions of high power are involved in sharing the charms of a buxom and skillful courtesan. Sometimes a courtesan should be generous to men in high positions for the sake of her safety and future.

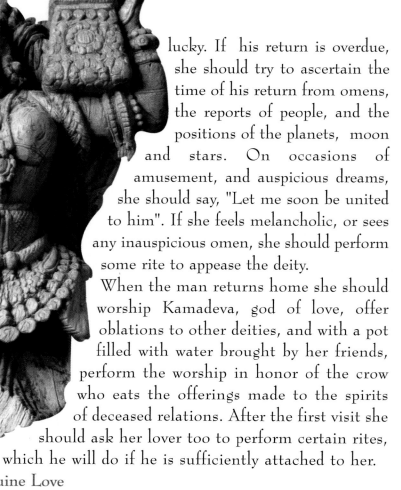

lucky. If his return is overdue, she should try to ascertain the time of his return from omens, the reports of people, and the positions of the planets, moon and stars. On occasions of amusement, and auspicious dreams, she should say, "Let me soon be united to him". If she feels melancholic, or sees any inauspicious omen, she should perform some rite to appease the deity.

When the man returns home she should worship Kamadeva, god of love, offer oblations to other deities, and with a pot filled with water brought by her friends, perform the worship in honor of the crow who eats the offerings made to the spirits of deceased relations. After the first visit she should ask her lover too to perform certain rites, which he will do if he is sufficiently attached to her.

Genuine Love

A man is said to be sufficiently attached to a woman when his love is disinterested; when he has the same object in view as his beloved; when he is free from any suspicions about her; and when he is indifferent to money with regard to her.

This is the manner of a courtesan living with a man like a wife, and set forth here for guidance from the rules of Dattaka. Anything not laid down here should be practiced according to the customs of the people, and the nature of each individual man.

Two *shlokas* on the subject elaborate:

The extent of the love of women is not known, even to those who are the objects of their affection, on account of its subtlety, and on account of the avarice, and natural intelligence of womankind.

Women are hardly ever known in their true light, though they may love men, or become indifferent towards them; may give them delight, or abandon them, or may extract from them all the wealth that they may possess.

ACQUIRING WEALTH

अर्थागमोपायप्रकरण

Arthagamopaya Prakarana

oney is obtained from a lover either by natural and lawful means, or by artifice. The ancient sages advised that if a courtesan can elicit abundant money from her lover, she should not make use of artifice. But Vatsyayana affirms that though she may get some money from him by natural means, yet when she makes use of artifice he gives her doubly more, and therefore, it should be resorted to for extorting money from him.

Extracting Money by Artifice

The artifices to be used for obtaining money from her lover are: taking money from him for the purchase of ornaments, food, drink, flowers, perfumes and clothes, and either not buy them or

(Left) A courtesan should never lead herself away from her prime objective, that is to acquire money from a lover, either by lawful means or by artifice.

buy them at a lower cost; praising his intelligence to his face, thereby obliging him to present gifts on festive occasions connected with vows, tree worship, garden parties, temple feasts and Holi - the festival of color; asserting falsely that her jewels have been forcibly taken by the king's guards or by robbers on her way to his house; alleging that her belongings have been destroyed by fire due to negligent servants; pretending to have lost his ornaments with her own; conveying to him through other people the expenses incurred by her in coming to see him; contracting debts for his sake; disputing with her mother about some expense incurred by her on his behalf; not attending parties in her friends' houses for lack of suitable presents, in return for their valuable presents to her; not performing certain festive rites due to lack of money; engaging artists to perform for him; and entertaining physicians and ministers who are important for attaining his objects.

Other methods of extracting money by artifice are: assisting friends and benefactors on festive occasions and in misfortune; paying the marriage expenses of a friend's son; recovering the cost of treatment of a pretended illness; satisfying abnormal desires during her pregnancy; giving her lover a valuable memento by selling some of her ornaments, furniture, or cooking utensils to a trader, well tutored in concealment; buying expensive cooking utensils more easily distinguishable than those of other people; remembering his former favors, and having them spoken of by friends and followers; telling him in glowing, exaggerated terms of the riches of rival

(Left) Adept at the art of giving sexual fulfillment, the young courtesan sits atop his erect lingam in a posture that provides him with a beautiful view of her rounded posteriors. He uses his legs to vigorously thrust upwards.

courtesans; describing to other courtesans, and in his presence, her own valuable possessions, and even falsely exaggerating their value; openly opposing her mother who is persuading her to reunite with former lovers who are richer; and lastly, extolling to her lover the liberality of his rivals.

Getting Rid of a Lover

A woman should always know her lover's state of mind, feelings, and disposition by the changes in his temper, manner, and facial expressions. A waning lover's behavior can be judged when he gives the woman less than is wanted, or something other than is asked for, false promises, building up her hopes, pretending to do something and doing otherwise; not fulfilling her wishes, forgetting his promises, speaking with his servants incoherently and mysteriously; and at every opportunity, sleeping in another house under some pretext.

When a courtesan finds that her lover's disposition towards her is changing, she should take possession of all his valuables before he becomes aware of her intentions, and allow a supposed creditor to take them away forcibly from her in satisfaction of a pretended debt. After this, if the lover is rich and has behaved well towards her, she should always treat him with respect; but if he becomes poor and destitute, she should free herself from him. Getting rid of a lover who is out of favor is achieved by denigrating his habits and vices as disagreeable and censurable, sneering and stamping her foot;

(Above and Right) A courtesan accompanied by musicians and a group of dancers displays her dancing skills in a lively performance in the king's court. Such performances reap handsome rewards in the form of money, gold and jewels.

speaking on a subject of which he is ignorant, scoffing at his learning, and thus belittling his pride; seeking the company of men who are superior to him in learning and wisdom, disregarding him on all occasions; censuring men with the same faults as his; expressing dissatisfaction at his methods of enjoyment, not letting him kiss her, refusing access to her bed and denying his rights to her body; showing a dislike for the wounds made by his nails and teeth, keeping completely still during forced congress, seducing him when he is fatigued and joking at his failure, while laughing at his attachment to her; not responding to his embraces by feigning sleep or going out visiting when he desires to enjoy her during the daytime. Other ways of belittling him are: misconstruing his words, and laughing without reason or at his jokes, looking with side glances at her own attendants, clapping at his statements, interrupting his stories, telling other stories, proclaiming his faults and vices as incurable; speaking disparagingly about him to her female attendants; not looking at him when he comes to her; asking him for what cannot be granted; and, after all, dismissing him.

There are some *shlokas* on this subject :

The duty of a courtesan consists in forming connections
with suitable men after due and full consideration, and
attaching the person with whom she is united to
herself; in obtaining wealth from the person attached to
her, and then dismissing him after she has taken away all
his possessions.

A courtesan leading in this manner the life of a
wife is not troubled with too many lovers, and yet
obtains abundance of wealth.

RECONCILIATION

विशीर्णप्रतिसन्धानप्रकरण

Vishirnapratisandhana Prakarana

When a courtesan abandons her present lover after his wealth is depleted, she may consider reunion with a former lover. But she should return to him only if he is wealthier than before, and if he is still attached to her. If, however, he is living with another woman, she must consider the position carefully.

Reuniting with a Former Lover

A former lover may have left the first woman of his own accord, and perhaps another woman since then, or have been driven away by both women. He may have been given up by one woman, or forsaken the other, or gone to live with another. Or he may have abandoned one woman of his own accord, and be living with another woman. If he has deserted both women, he should not be entertained due to his fickleness and indifference to both of them. If the man driven away by both women has been turned away by

---

(Left) If a former lover, turned away by the courtesan wishes to reunite with her, she should determine his intentions: whether or not he still has any affection for her, and would consequently spend money upon her. If after mature consideration, she finds his intentions to be really upright, she can reconcile with him.

नीकरासनः

the second because she could get more money from another man, then he should be resorted to by the first woman because he would then give her more money, through vanity and spite. But if both women have turned him away due to his poverty or stinginess, he should not be thought of. If the man who has given up one woman, and been driven away by the other, and if he agrees to return to the former and gives her plenty of money beforehand, then he should be approached.

As for the man who may have left one woman, and is living with another, the former, wishing to take up with him again, should first ascertain if he left her because of some particular excellence in the other woman, and not having found it, is willing to come back to her, and give her enough money to make up for his conduct, and his continuing affection. Or, having discovered many faults in the other woman, he would now see even better qualities in her than actually exist, and be prepared to give her money for these apparent qualities.

Lastly, the woman should consider whether he was weak-minded, enjoyed many women, or never did anything for the woman that he was with, and then decide if she should accept him or not, according to circumstances.

Gauging His Intentions

If the woman turned away the man, who was subsequently abandoned by another, and wishes to reunite with him, she should

The young maiden playfully places one leg around her lover's waist in an attempt to climb onto him.(Pages 270-271) The woman lies down in the crab's position with her thighs contracted, and placed on her stomach and her legs up in the air and provides an easy entrance to her heavenly abode. (Left) Heavenly maidens, descending from the sky were often used by the gods to distract sages from their penance.

determine his intentions: whether he still has any affection for her, and would consequently spend much money upon her; or appreciates her excellent qualities and did not take delight in any other women; was driven away before satisfying his sexual desires, and wishes to return to her, to avenge the injury done to him; whether he wishes to inspire her confidence to recover the wealth she had acquired from him; or, lastly, whether he wishes to separate her from her present lover, and then break away from her himself. If after mature consideration, she finds his intentions to be really upright, she can reconcile with him. However, if his mind is still tainted with evil intentions, he should be avoided.

If the man, driven away by one woman, and living with another, makes overtures to return to the former, the courtesan should consider well before she acts, and while the other woman is engaged in attracting him, she should try to win him over secretly for any of these reasons: that he was driven away unjustly, and since every effort must be made to bring him back from the other woman, she should converse with him again to separate from the other woman; to diminish the pride of her present lover; the former has become wealthy, secured a higher position, with a place of authority under the king; he is separated from his wife; is independent, and lives apart from his father or brother; that by making peace with him, she will be able to get hold of a very rich man, who is being prevented from approaching her by her present lover; that since he is no longer respected by his wife, she would now be able to separate him from her; that his friend loves her rival, who, in turn, hates

An over indulging patron dalliances with two women at the same time. (Right) An influential and wealthy courtesan has many attendants to take care of her needs.

the courtesan, and she would be able to separate the friend from his mistress. Lastly, winning him back would show his fickleness and bring discredit upon him.

Luring Back a Former Lover

When a courtesan is resolved to take up again with a former lover, her *pithamarda* and other servants should tell him that his expulsion from the woman's house was caused by the wickedness of her mother; the woman loved him but had to defer to her mother's will; she hated her present lover, and disliked him excessively. In addition, they should make him confident of her former love for him, and allude to the mark of that love that she has ever remembered which is connected with some kind of pleasure practiced by him, such as his way of kissing her, or having sexual intercourse.

When a woman has to choose between two lovers, one of whom was formerly united with her, while the other is a stranger, the *acharyas, sages,* are of the opinion that the first one is preferable; since his disposition and character are already known by previous careful observation, he can be easily pleased and satisfied. But Vatsyayana

thinks that a former lover, having already spent a great deal of his wealth, is not able or willing to give much money again, and is, therefore, not to be relied upon as much as a stranger. Cases may however differ on account of the different natures of men.

Some *shlokas* aver:

Reunion with a former lover may be desirable so as to separate some particular woman from some particular man, or some particular man from some particular woman, or to have a certain effect upon the present lover.

When a man is excessively attached to a woman, he is afraid of her coming into contact with other men; he does not then regard or notice her faults and he gives her much wealth through fear of her leaving him.

A courtesan should be agreeable to the man who is attached to her, and despise the man who does not care for her. If while she is living with one man, a messenger comes to her from some other man, she may either refuse to listen to any negotiations on his part, or appoint a fixed time for him to visit her, but she should not leave the man who may be living with her and who may be attached to her.

A wise woman should only renew her connection with a former lover, if she is satisfied that good fortune, gain, love, and friendship are likely to be the result of such a reunion.

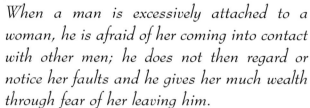

A courtesan, well dressed and wearing ornaments, should stand at the door of her house to be seen by people on the road, since she is like an object on view for sale.

SPECIAL GAINS

लाभविशेषप्रकरण

Labhavishesha Prakarana

hen a courtesan is able to realize much money every day from numerous customers, she should not confine herself to a single lover. Under such circumstances, she should fix her rate for one night, after considering the place, season, people, her own beauty and good qualities, and the comparative rates of other courtesans. She can then inform her lovers, friends, and acquaintances about her charges. If, however, she can obtain this from a single lover, she may resort to him alone, and live with him as if she had been solely reserved for him.

Gold Is the Most Valuable

The sages are of the opinion that when a courtesan can gain equally from two lovers at the same time, she should give preference to the one who would give her what she wants. But Vatsyayana asserts that preference should be given to the one who gives her gold, because it cannot be taken back like other things; it can be easily received, and can procure anything wished for. Gold is superior to silver, copper, bell-metal, iron, pots, furniture, beds, upper garments, under vestments, fragrant substances, vessels made of gourds, ghee, oil, corn, cattle, and other such items.

Choosing between Two Lovers

When the same effort is required to win over any two lovers, or when both will give her the same kind of comforts, the choice should be made on a friend's advice, or on their personal qualities, or signs of good or bad fortune connected with them.

Of two lovers, one of whom is attached to the courtesan, and the other is merely very generous, the sages say preference should be given to the generous lover. But Vatsyayana is of the opinion that the one who is really attached to the courtesan should be preferred because he can be made to be generous, even as a miser gives money if he becomes fond of a woman; but a man who is simply generous cannot be made to love with real attachment. But if two lovers are attached to her, and there is a choice between one who is poor, and one who is rich, the preference is of course to be given to the rich lover.

When there are two lovers, one of whom is generous, and the other ready to do any service for the courtesan, some sages say the latter should be preferred. But in Vatsyayana's opinion such a man thinks he has gained his object by performing this service once, but a generous man does not care for what he has given before. Even here the choice should be guided by the likelihood of the future good to be derived from her union with either of them.

When one lover is grateful, and the other liberal, some sages say the liberal one should be preferred, but Vatsyayana affirms that the former should be chosen, because liberal men being generally haughty, plain-spoken, and inconsiderate, do not care for long friendships or past services, and leave abruptly if they see any fault in the courtesan, or are told lies about her by another woman. On the other hand the grateful man does not break off from her at once, because of his regard for the pains she may have taken to please him. Here too the choice should depend on the future.

(Left) The mischievous nayika, *full of flirtatious exuberance seduces a sage by embracing him.*

When there is a choice between complying with the request of a friend, or a chance of getting money, the sages say the latter should be preferred. But Vatsyayana believes that money can be obtained tomorrow as well as today, and, therefore, the future good should be considered before disregarding a friend's request. But on such an occasion, the courtesan could pacify her friend by pretending to be busy and promising to comply with his request the next day, and thus, also obtain the money offered to her.

When there is a choice between getting money and avoiding a disaster, the sages suggest the former. Vatsyayana disagrees and asserts that money only has a limited importance, while a disaster once averted may never occur again. The choice should be guided by the potential size of the disaster.

Use of Wealth by Courtesans for Piety
The riches of the ganikas, the wealthiest and best kind of courtesans, are to be spent in building temples, water-tanks, and gardens; giving a thousand cows to different Brahmins; worshipping the gods, celebrating festivals in their honor; and lastly performing such vows as may be within their means.

Other courtesans should spend their acquired wealth on wearing a a clean dress every day; sufficient food and

By using their skills in the art of giving pleasure two experienced courtesans entertain a highly virile group of young men. (Right) A 14th century miniature from the manuscript Laur Chanda. *The two lovers escape with the help of her maid and a lax guard.*

drink to satisfy hunger and thirst; eating a perfumed *tambula*, a mixture of betel nut and betel leaves daily; and wearing gilt ornaments. The sages say these represent the gains of all the middle and lower classes of courtesans, but Vatsyayana says that these cannot be calculated as they depend on the influence of the place, the customs of the people, their appearance, and other indefinable things.

When to Forego or Extract Money

A courtesan should forego a great reward and agree to take only a small sum of money in a friendly way from a man if she wishes to keep him from other women; get him away from some woman to whom he is attached; deprive some woman of her acquired riches; raise her position; enjoy some great good fortune; become desirable to all men by uniting herself with him; wishes for his assistance to avert some misfortune; is really attached to him; wishes to injure somebody through his influence; remembers some former favor conferred upon her; or wishes to be united with him merely from desire.

When a courtesan intends to abandon a particular lover, and take up with another; or believes he will shortly leave her, and return to his wives; or having squandered all his money and become penniless, he will be taken away by his guardian, or master, or father; or he is about to lose his position; or he is very fickle, she should endeavor to get as much money as she can from him as soon as possible.

On the other hand, when the courtesan thinks her lover is about to receive valuable presents; or is expecting his ship laden with merchandise; or is to get a place of authority from the king; or is soon to inherit a fortune; or has large stocks of corn and other commodities; or will regard with favor anything done for him; or is always true to his word; then should she have regard to her future welfare, and live with him like his wife.

(Left) Two frisky and sportive mates take delight in recreating with a highly buxom and voluptuous Hastini nayika.

Some *shlokas* state:

In considering her present gains, and her future welfare, a courtesan should avoid such persons as have gained their means of subsistence with very great difficulty, as also those who have become selfish and hard-hearted by becoming the favorites of kings.

She should make every endeavor to unite herself with prosperous and well-to-do people, and with those whom it is dangerous to avoid, or to slight in any way. Even at some cost to herself she should become acquainted with energetic and liberal-minded men, who when pleased would give her a large sum of money, even for very little service, or for some small thing.

An intoxicated courtesan sits in an inviting pose with her legs wide apart. (Left) One of the 2nd century Begram Ivories portrays two full-hipped, narrow-waisted courtesans, decked with heavy jewellery.

Gains and losses

अर्थानर्थानुबन्धसंशयविचारप्रकरण

Arthanarthanubandhasanshayavichara Prakarana

G ain is of three kinds: gain of wealth, religious merit and pleasure; similarly, loss is of three kinds: loss of wealth, religious merit and pleasure.

Causes of Losses

Sometimes when gains are being sought, or expected to be realized, the efforts result in losses. The causes of are many and varied: weakness of intellect, simplicity, excessive love, pride, over-confidence, self-conceit, excessive anger, carelessness, recklessness, evil genius, and unavoidable and unfortunate circumstances. This results in unnecessary expense, destruction of future good fortune, loss of potential gains and what one has, an uncertain temper, and loss of health, hair, and happiness.

When a gain is sought and other gains are also acquired, these are attendant gains. When gain is uncertain, it is termed as a simple doubt. When there is a doubt about two possible results, it is a mixed doubt. If for one action there are two results, it is a

---

(Left) A courtesan should make every endeavor to unite with prosperous and liberal minded people, whom when pleased, would give her large sums of money even for a very little service.

combination of two results, and if several results follow the same action, it is a combination of results of every side.

By living with a great man, if a courtesan acquires wealth and becomes acquainted with other people, a chance of future fortune, accession of wealth, and becomes desirable to all, this is a double gain of wealth and future fortune.

If by living with a man a courtesan only gets money, this is just a gain of wealth without any complications.

When a courtesan receives money from other people besides her lover, the results are: the possible loss of future good from her present lover; the disaffection of a man securely attached to her; the hatred of all; and a probable union with some low person, which could destroy her future. This is a gain of wealth attended by losses.

When a courtesan, at her own expense and without any tangible gain, has a connection with a great man, or an avaricious minister, for the sake of diverting some misfortune or removing some obstacle threatening the destruction of a great gain, this is said to be a loss of wealth attended by gains of future good.

A courtesan who is kind, even at her own expense, to a man who is very stingy, proud of his looks, or ungrateful but attractive to women, suffers a loss of wealth unattended by any gain.

When she is kind to such a man, who in addition is a favorite of the king, and cruel and powerful, without any good resulting from it, and a chance of her suddenly being turned away, this is a loss of wealth together with other losses.

Similarly secondary gains and losses in religious merit and pleasures

(Above and Right) Courtesans skilled in the art of dancing can easily find followers.

also become apparent, and combinations of all of them can be made.

Doubts: Monetary, Ethical, and Erotic

Doubts are again of three kinds: about wealth, religious merit, and pleasures. When a courtesan is not certain how much a man may give her, or spend on her, she has a doubt about wealth.

When she is doubtful whether she is right in entirely abandoning a lover from whom she is unable to get money, having taken all his wealth from him earlier, this is a doubt about morality.

When she is unable to get a lover of her liking, and is uncertain about deriving any pleasure from a person surrounded by his family, or from a low person, this is a doubt about pleasure.

When a courtesan is uncertain whether a powerful but principled man would cause her loss if she is uncivil to him, this is a doubt about the loss of wealth.

If she abandons a man attached to her without showing him the slightest favor, causing him unhappiness in this world and the next, this is a doubt about the loss of religious merit.

If she is burning with desire but uncertain of her lover's arrival and being satisfied, this is a doubt about the loss of pleasure.

The connection with a newcomer of unknown disposition, who was recommended by a lover, or by one in authority, may be productive either of gain or loss, and is, therefore, a mixed doubt about the gain and loss of wealth.

A courtesan requested by a friend, or impelled by compassion to have intercourse with a learned Brahmin, a religious student, a devotee, or an ascetic who have all fallen in love with her, and are besotted enough to threaten suicide, suffers an uncertainty about the gain and loss of religious merit.

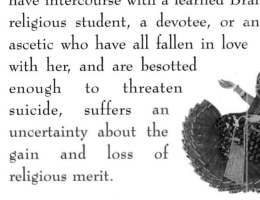

If a courtesan relies solely upon hearsay and rumor about a man, and goes to him without ascertaining for herself whether he has good or bad qualities, and the likely result, this is a mixed doubt about the gain and loss of pleasure.

Auddalika has described the gains and losses on both sides in a concise manner: if a courtesan, living with a lover, gets both wealth and pleasure from him, it is a gain on both sides.

When a courtesan lives with a lover at her own expense without any profit, and the lover even takes back what he has given her earlier, it is a loss on both sides.

When a courtesan is uncertain of a new acquaintance becoming attached to her, and whether he would give her anything, it is a doubt on both sides about gains.

If a courtesan is uncertain whether a former enemy, befriended again at her own expense, would cause her harm because of his grudge against her; or angrily take away anything previously given to her, this is a doubt on both sides about loss.

Babhravya has described the gain and loss on both sides thus: when a courtesan can get money from a man whom she may go to see, and money from a man whom she may not go to see, this is a gain on both sides.

This painting from South India depicts a couple in a sensuous and fleshy display of their sexual talents. (Left) The couple is engage in a variation of the suspended congress, where the bejeweled enchantress knots her legs in a posture, which would require yogic expertise.

When a courtesan has to incur further expense if she goes to see a man, but runs the risk of incurring an irremediable loss if she does not, this is a loss on both sides.

Where a courtesan is uncertain about a particular man giving her anything if she visits him, without incurring any expense, or whether by neglecting him, another man would give her something, this is a doubt on both sides about gain.

When a courtesan is uncertain whether, on visiting an old enemy at her own expense, he would take back what he had given her, or if by not going he would cause her harm, this is a doubt on both sides about loss.

When a courtesan consorts with men she should make them give her money as well as pleasure. (Right) During long lasting wars, soldiers on duty and fighting for their kingdoms, away from their homes often took along a battery of courtesans for pleasure and entertainment.

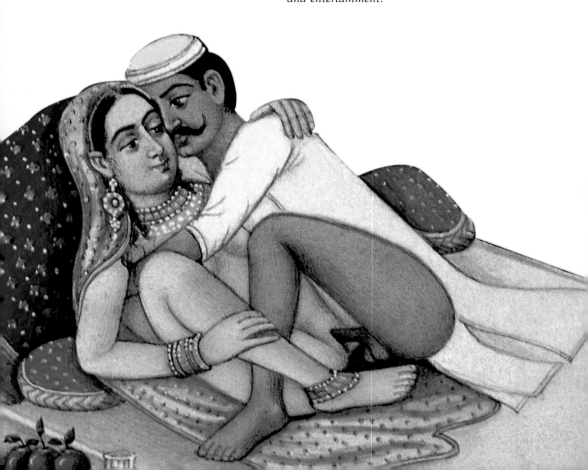

Forming New Combinations

Having considered this and taken the counsel of her friends, a courtesan should act with the objective of acquiring wealth and warding off disaster. Religious merit and pleasure should also be formed into separate combinations like those of wealth, and then regrouped with each other to make new combinations.

When a courtesan consorts with men she should make them give her money as well as pleasure. On special occasions, such as the Spring Festival, her mother should announce to the various men that her daughter will spend a certain day with the man who would gratify a particular desire of hers.

When young men approach her with delight, she should think of what she may accomplish through them.

A courtesan should also consider doubts about gain and loss with reference to wealth, religious merit, and pleasure.

The different kinds of prostitute are: *kulata* and *swairini*, secret and open adulteress, *kumbha-dasi*, a common whore, *paricharika*, female attendant, *nati*, an actress or dancing girl, *shilpa-karika*, an artisan, *prakasha*, deserter-wife, *rupajiva*, one with a beautiful body, and *ganika*, a courtesan.

All these prostitutes are acquainted with various kinds of men, and should consider ways of getting money from them, pleasing them, separating from them, and re-uniting. They should also consider particular gains and losses, attendant gains and losses, and doubts in accordance with their own conditions.

Two *shlokas* on the subject state:

Men want pleasure, while women want money, and therefore this part, which treats of the means of gaining wealth, should be studied.

There are some women who seek for love, and there are others who seek for money; for the former the ways of love are told in previous portions of this work, while the ways of getting money, as practiced by courtesans, are described in this part.

Two gracefully entangled and excited lovers display the woman on top posture. (Left) The extraordinarily flexible torso of the seductress allows for an almost impossible posture. The posture requires great strength and suppleness in the participants' bodies.

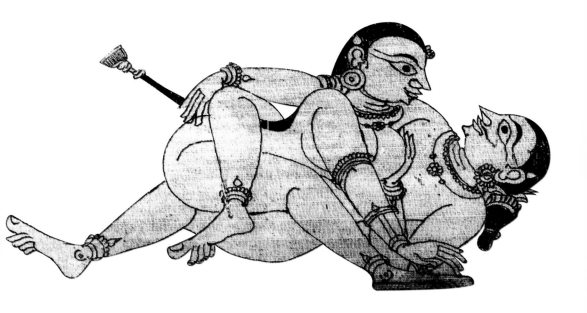

Secret Lore, Extraneous Stimulation, and Sexual Power

Beautifying the body

Regarding virility

Book 7

BEAUTIFYING THE body

सुभगंकरणादिप्रकरण

Subhagankaranadi Prakarana

f one fails to attain the heart's desire by any of the methods described earlier, one can take recourse to different means of attracting others to accomplish the fulfillment of inner passions. One's fortune is also considerably improved by adopting the special measures described in the *Tantra Shastra* and the *Atharva Veda*.

Secret Formulae to Enhance Beauty

Good looks, good qualities, youth and liberality are the principal and most natural means of making a person agreeable in others' eyes. But in their absence, a man or woman can resort to secret recipes, charms, aphrodisiacs, artificial membranes and the artful application of cosmetics. Some recipes for these may be useful.

A paste made from the leaves of *tagara*, *kashtha*, and *talisapatra*, smeared all over the body increases physical beauty.

If a fine power made of the same plants is made into a wick mixed with *bibhitaka* oil and ignited, the result is *kohl*, eye-black. Applied

---

(Left) A group of ascetics and mendicants are engaged in the preparation of various medicines, mixtures and aphrodisiacs for enhancement of sexual pleasure.

to the eyelashes, this enlarges the appearance of the eyes, and makes the face most attractive.

The roots of *punarnava, sahadevi, sariva,* and *kurantaka* should be boiled with the leaves of *utpala,* in oil of sesamum. This oil massaged all over the body enhances the texture and sheen of the skin. A thick paste of these ingredients made into beads and worn as a garland at the same time, intensifies the effect.

If the stamen of the flowers of *padma* and *utpala,* white and blue lotus, together with *nagakesara,* is dried, powdered and mixed with honey and clarified butter, and sipped, it improves the complexion. If together with the oral concoction, the body is smeared with a paste of these ingredients, mixed with the powder of *tagara, talisa,* and *tamalapatra,* the effect is doubly augmented.

Efficacious and beautifying amulets are also recommended. A powerful talisman is the eye of a peacock sealed into a golden case at an auspicious moment. Other amulets are dried berries or the *badaramani,* gathered from the topmost branches, the stones removed and sorted. If a berry with a right hand opening like a *shankhamani,* conch, is found, it is most propitious and being very rare, should be consecrated by hymns from the *Atharva Veda,* by a skilled yogi adept in the science of magic.

Giving a Courtesan's Daughter in Marriage

When a female attendant reaches the age of puberty, her master should keep her isolated, and when young men ardently desire her because of her seclusion, and the difficulty of approaching her, he should bestow her hand on such a man as may endow her with wealth to prevent a rival from getting the better of him. This is a recognized means of increasing the maid's good fortune and happiness, the attributes of attractiveness and a loving nature.

Similarly, when a courtesan's daughter reaches the age of puberty, the mother should get together many young men of the same age, disposition, and knowledge as her daughter, and tell them she would give her in *panigrahana,* holding of the hands ceremony, to the boy who would give her presents of a valuable kind. After this the daughter is kept in seclusion as far as possible, and then given to the youth ready to give her the presents agreed upon. If the mother is unable to get so much out of him, she should display some of her own possessions as having been given to the daughter by her lover.

Or the mother may allow her daughter to be attached to her lover privately, while feigning ignorance; then pretending it has come to her knowledge, give her consent.

The daughter, too, should attract the sons of wealthy citizens, unknown to her mother, and make them regard her with affection. She should meet them when learning to sing, in places where music is played, and the houses of other people; then request her mother, through a female friend or servant, to be allowed to unite with the young man most agreeable to her.

When a courtesan's daughter is thus given to a lover, the

When an ointment made of kokilaksha *fruit is applied to the yoni of a Hastini woman, her yoni will contract for one night. (Left) By drinking milk mixed with certain ayurvedic ingredients a man can increase his sexual vigor and can become as virile as animals.*

relationship is to be observed for one year, and after that she is free to do what she likes. But even after the end of the year, if she is occasionally invited by her first consort to come and visit him, when otherwise engaged, she should go to him for the night.

Such is the mode of temporary union among courtesans, and of

increasing their loveliness, and their value in the eyes of others. The same also applies to the daughters of dancing women, who should give them only to such persons as are likely to be useful to them in various ways.

Compelling Love and Enslaving Others

There are means of attracting others and raising one's prowess to enviable heights. If a man anoints his *lingam* with a mixture of the powders of *dhatturaka,* white thorn apple, *pippali,* long pepper, *maricha,* black pepper, and *madhu,* honey, and engages in sexual union with a woman, he makes her subject to his will.

An application of a mixture of the *vatodbhranta patra* leaves scattered by the wind, the flowers thrown on a human corpse to be burnt, and the powdered bones of the *mayura,* peacock, and *jivanjivaka,* swallow bird, enables the man to sexually satisfy the woman completely.

A paste made from the powdered remains of a kite which has died a natural death, cowdung ash and honey, if applied to the body before taking a bath, will enable the man to attract any woman.

Anointing the phallus with a salve made of the *amalaka* plant enhances the power of subjecting women to one's will.

A man who grinds the sprouts of the *vajrasruhi* into small pieces and dips them into a mixture of red arsenic and pure sulphur, dries them seven times, and applies this mixed with honey to his *lingam,* can subjugate a woman to his will during sexual union, or, if he burns these sprouts at night and sees a golden moon behind the smoke, he will be successful with any woman. If he mixes the powder of these sprouts with the excreta of a monkey, and throws this on a maiden, she will not be easily attached to anybody else.

If pieces of *Vacha* are dressed with *amra-tailam,* mango oil, and preserved for six months in a crevice in the forked trunk of the *shimshapa,* sissu tree, and are then made into a paste, and applied to the *lingam* before engaging in sexual union, this will subjugate women.

A camel bone dipped into the juice of *bharingaraj* is burnt, and the black pigment from its ashes placed in a box made of camel bone, and applied together with *anjana,* antimony, to the eyelashes with a sliver of camel bone. This pigment is said to be very pure and wholesome for the eyes, and subjugates others to the will of the person who uses it.

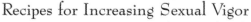

Recipes for Increasing Sexual Vigor

Men can increase sexual vigor by drinking milk mixed with sugar, the powdered root of *uchchaata, chavya,* and *yashtimadhuka,* liquorice, and become as virile as bulls.

Drinking milk, in which the testicles of a ram or a goat have been boiled and mixed with sugar, increases sexual stamina.

Seeds of long pepper with sugarcane roots, and *vidari,* pounded

(Left and above) If one fails to attain the heart's desire, one can take recourse to different means of attracting others to accomplish the fulfillment of inner passions. Some of these measures find their base in the Tantra Shastra.

together and mixed with milk, act as a powerful stimulant.

If the seeds or roots of *sringataka, kaseruka,* and liquorice are pounded with *kshirakakoli,* a kind of onion, and the powder is put into milk mixed with sugar and clarified butter, and boiled on a moderate fire, the man who drinks this syrup will be able to enjoy innumerable women.

Similarly, if a man mixes rice with the eggs of a sparrow, boils this in milk, adds clarified butter and honey, and drinks it, he will enhance his sexual ability.

If a man soaks the outer covering of sesamum seeds with the eggs of sparrows, boils them in milk, mixed with sugar and clarified butter, adds the fruits of *sringataka* and the *kaseruka* plant, wheat flour and *swayamgupta* beans, and then drinks this concoction, he can enjoy countless women.

If equal quantities of clarified butter, honey, sugar, and liquorice, the juice of the fennel plant, and milk are mixed together, this nectar-like composition is said to be holy, provocative of sexual vigour, a preserver of life, and sweet to the taste.

Tonics for Health and Longevity

Extracts of *shatavari,* with *shvadamshtra* are mixed with treacle and boiled in thickened cow's milk with clarified butter; long pepper, liquorice, and honey are added, making a concoction delightful to taste. Taken every day starting when the moon enters the *Pushya* constellation, this is conducive to

Tantric art provides for unique and unusual imagery. (Left) Specific tantras are devoted to the mode of ritual of worship of Goddess Kali and the benefits that are to be gained from the worship. Here Kali stands stride Kama and Rati, the feminine and masculine principles lying conjoined beneath her feet and representing female ascendancy for the sake of creation.

longevity and recuperative after excesses.

Boiling *shatavari* and *shvadamshtra* with the pounded fruits of *shriparni*, in water, and drinking this every day, is a recuperative tonic. Drinking boiled clarified butter in the morning during the spring, benefits health by providing strength, and is agreeable to the taste. If the powdered seeds of *gokshura* and barley flour are mixed in equal parts, and two *palas* of this in weight eaten every morning on waking up, it is beneficial.

If equal amounts of *shatavari, gokshura,* and *shriparni* are macerated, boiled in water and strained, the mixture is a powerful tonic for toning up the body and enhancing vigor. It should be taken in the cool weather every morning.

There are also *shlokas* on the subject :

The means of producing love and sexual vigor should be learned from the science of medicine, from the Atharva Veda, the Tantra Shastras, and those who are learned in the arts of magic, and experienced alchemists. No means should be employed which are doubtful in their effects, likely to cause injury to the body, which involve the death of animals, and which bring us in contact with impure things. Such means should only be used as are holy, acknowledged to be good and approved of by Brahmins and friends.

A woman's passion is often insatiable and artificial phalluses as also appendages wrapped around the lingam *are invaluable. They have the effect of inciting fiery sexual urges in the highly passionate woman and then she can be satisfied. (Pages 308-309) A horse having once attained the fifth degree of motion, goes on with blind speed, regardless of pits, ditches and posts in his way. In the same manner copulation having once commenced, passion alone gives birth to the act of all parties. Here the artist paints groups of lovers blinded by desire and making furious love.*

REGARdiNG viRiliTy

नष्टरागप्रत्यानयनप्रकरण

Nashtaragapratyanayana Prakarana

 man unable to relieve the sexual urges of an intensely passionate woman, should take recourse to various means to excite her passion. One way of exciting a woman is to manipulate her *yoni* with his hand or fingers, and not begin intercourse with her until she becomes excited, or experiences pleasure; then he should introduce his phallus so that her orgasm precedes his ejaculation.

Kinds of Sexual Tools

Alternatively, he may make use of certain *apadravyas*, phallus-shaped artificial gadgets, pierced only at the top, to be put on or around the *lingam* supplementing its length or its thickness to fit into the *yoni*. In Babhravya's opinion, these *apadravyas* should be made of gold, silver, copper, iron, ivory, buffalo's horn, wood, tin or lead, and should be soft, cool, provocative of sexual vigor, and well fitted like a ring or a glove to serve the intended purpose and be capable of withstanding vigorous action. Vatsyayana, however, states that these may be made according to the natural choice of each individual.

The different kinds of *apadravyas* are: the *valaya*, ring, made of the

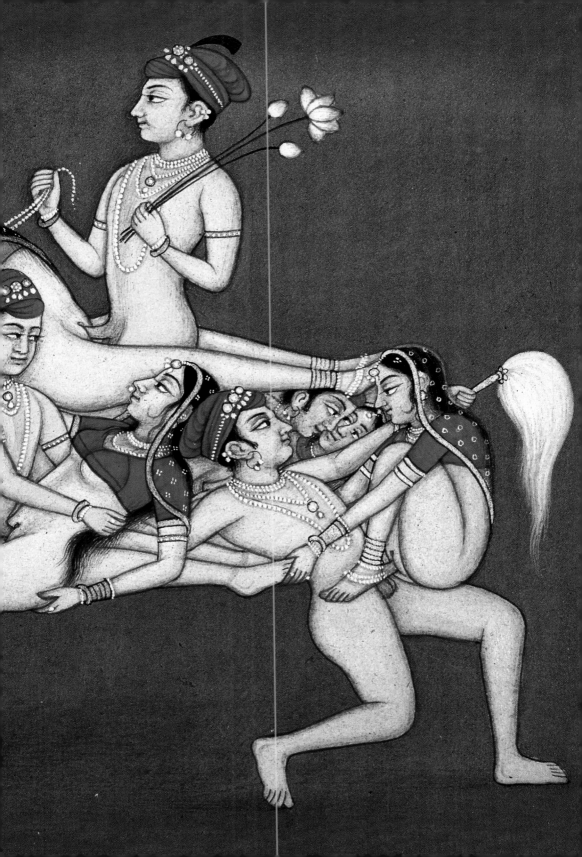

same size as the *lingam,* its outer surface uneven with ridges and worn around it like an amulet; the *sanghati,* couple, formed of two rings placed over the *lingam;* the *chudaka,* bracelet, made by joining three or more rings, until they come up to the required length of the *lingam;* and the *ekachudaka,* single bracelet, formed by wrapping a single band around the *lingam,* according to the required dimensions.

An artificial phallus aid such as the *kanchuka,* closed sheath, and *jalaka,* latticed net open at the tip, should be the size of the erect member which is to be inserted into it; cavities for the testicles will enhance the overall effect. Outwardly somewhat rough with nodules to fit the size of the *yoni* to enhance the woman's coital pleasure, it can be kept in position by tying it to the hips.

In the absence of such *apadravyas,* a phallic tube may be made from the stem of the *alabu,* bottlegourd, or the *venu,* bamboo; according to the size desired, it should be well seasoned in medicated oil before use and tied to the waist with thread.

Young men, indeed men of all ages, are afflicted with impaired virility, premature ejaculation, partial tumescence, and a slow rise in passion, due to excess or over- indulgence. Fellatio, or oral sex, will induce full tumescence and make normal coitus possible. The acceleration of passion is also achieved by manually effecting erection, aided by digital anal manipulation; nevertheless, the women's passion is often insatiable and artificial phalluses are therefore invaluable, as also the appendages wrapped around or put onto the *lingam;* besides the very act of tying them on to the erect penis, or the stone of the *amalaka* to the base of the organ, and the use of any of the aids described will have the effect of inciting the fiery sexual urges in the highly passionate woman, and she can then be satisfied.

(Right) Kali with companions from a Tantric Devi series. The goddess herself rests on a corpse as if on a throne. One of the companions lofts a flywhisk, an old age Indian symbol of attendance on the royal and divine.

Enlarging the Orifice of the Phallus

The people of the Deccan and the southern provinces contend that it is only possible to derive true sexual pleasure if the orifice of the *lingam* has been enlarged by perforation with a suitable, pointed shaft inserted into the opening at the tip of the glans penis and worked up and down so as to engorge the canal. This practice can be effected in childhood at the age when the ears are pierced.

A grown young man can also enlarge the aperture of his *lingam* with a thick wedge long enough to insert into the canal; the youth should stand in water as long as the wound bleeds,and the flow of blood with lessen with time. To prevent the enlarged aperture from contracting, he should engage in sexual intercourse with vigour, even if painful, to clear the orifice. Afterwards, the wound should be washed and cleaned frequently with an astringent decoction, and the hole increased in size by the gradual insertion of thicker and thicker wedges. The widened orifice should be simultaneously

cleaned with a paste made of *yashtimadhuka,* liquorice, and honey mixed with *kashayas;* the widening process can be continued by inserting *karnika* or *shishapatra* sticks anointed liberally with the oil of *bhallataka.*

In the enlarged orifice made in the *lingam,* the youth may insert various artificial aids of different shapes and sizes. They may be in the shape of a phallic head fully rounded at the end like a wooden pestle, a bud about to bloom; a proboscis; trunk of an elephant, an eight-sided variety; shaped like a top, a flat disc, or umbrella; *shringataka,* triangular; an assembly of balls; a gadget with locks of hair, and a type described as a crossroad where four roads meet. There are many others, named accordingly to their forms and means of using them. They may be rough or smooth, and are usually selected by young lovers according to their desires and needs, and most of all the appeal they make to the eyes of the beholder, and the resultant arousal of sexual impulses.

Enlarging the Phallus

To enlarge the *lingam* and make it strong, a variety of insects with irritating hair on their bodies, like the *kandalika,* a type of caterpillar, are removed from the trees on which they thrive, and vigorously rubbed on the

In the enlarged orifice made in the lingam *a youth may insert artificial aids of different shapes and sizes. They appeal to the eyes of the beholder and result in arousal of sexual impulses. (Left) A virile holy man takes advantage of his position and plays with the charms of a beautiful village belle.*

skin and prepuce of the phallus, which results in painful swelling. To allay the pain a soothing oil is rubbed all over the organ for at least ten successive nights, after which the insects are applied again, followed by the further application of oil. When in this process, the *lingam* has swollen considerably, its length can also be increased by lying on a rope bed and allowing it to hang downwards through a hole in the woven rope. When it is as large as possible, the *lingam* should be bathed in soothing extracts of herbs and oils. This enlargement of the phallus will last for life and is popular among the youth of Dravida; the *vitas* call it *shukashopha,* swollen and lengthened in size.

The *lingam* can be enlarged for one month by rubbing into the skin appropriate vesicants such as the juice of *ashvagandha,* the root of *shabara,* the fruit of *brihati,* and the root of *jalashuka.* Butter made from buffalo's milk with *hastikarna,* and *vajaravalli* will effect a good-sized swelling. The phallus can be enlarged for at least six months by massaging it with oil in which *kashayas* or any of these ingredients have been boiled; or by rubbing or moistening it with oil boiled on a moderate fire with the seeds of pomegranate, and a mixture of the juices of *baluka,* cucumber, and fruits of the

The five faced and ten armed Shiva with the fifth head unseen at the back was worshiped at the main temple in Mandi, North India. (Right) The Great Goddess Kali slaying demons in a vivid depiction of horrific power.

hastikarna plant and the eggplant. In addition, other means may be learned from experienced persons and confidants.

Miscellaneous Experiments and Love Potions

The mixture of powdered *snuhikantaka,* thorns of the milk-hedge plant, *punarnava,* and excreta of a monkey, together with the powdered root of *langalika,* thrown on the head of a woman, will make her love no one else.

The thickened juice of *somalata, avalguja, bhringaraja, vyadhighata,* and *jambu* fruit, applied to a woman's *yoni* before sex, results in the man's aversion to her.

If a woman bathes in the buttermilk of a she-buffalo, mixed with powders of the *gopalika, bahupadika,* and *jivhika* plants, she will lose the affection of the man.

A garland or paste prepared from the flowers of *kadamaba, amrataka,* and *jambu,* that is used by a woman, will bring her misfortune.

When an ointment made of the fruit of *kokilaksha* is applied to the *yoni* of a *Hastini,* elephant woman, her *yoni* will contract for one night.

When a paste made by pounding the roots of *padma* and *utpala,* white and blue lotus, and the powder of *sarjaka* and *sugandha,* with clarified butter and honey, is applied to the *yoni* of the *Mrigi,* deer woman, it will expand.

A mixture made of the *avalguja* fruit, soaked in the milky juice of the milk-hedge, *soma* and *snuhi* plants, and the juice of the *amalaka* fruit, will make the hair fair.

The juice of the roots of the *madayantika,* the yellow amaranth, the *anjanika, girikarnika* and *shlakshnaparni* plants, used as lotion, will make the hair grow rich and dark. A decoction made by boiling these roots in oil, and massaging it into the scalp will make the hair black, and will also gradually restore hair growth.

If *alaktaka* is saturated seven times in the sweat of the testicle of a white horse, and applied to a red lip, the lip will become pale.

The colour of the lips can be reddened by *madayantika* and other herbal ingredients.

A woman who hears a man playing on a reed pipe which has been dipped into the juices of the *bahupadika, kushtha, tagara, talisa,* and *vajrakanda* plants is enslaved by him.

Food mixed with the fruit of *dathura,* thorn apple, causes intoxication.

Eating lumps of jaggery which has been preserved for a long time restores steadiness of mind.

Water mixed with oil and the ashes of any kind of grass except *kusha* grass, becomes the color of milk.

Yellow myrabolans, hog plum, and *shrawana*

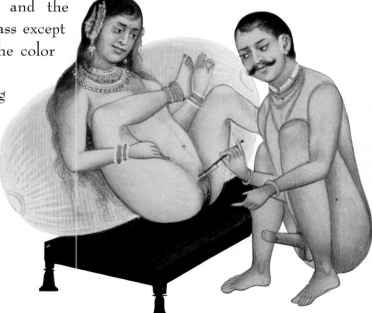

When a paste made by pounding the roots of certain ayurvedic plants with clarified butter and honey is applied to the yoni of a Mrigi, deer woman, it will expand.
(Left) The painting is representative of a relationship connotative as the Linga-yoni, male-female union, symbolically revered by Tantric devotees.

priyangu plants, all pounded together and applied to iron pots, oxidizes them red, like copper.

Drinking the milk of a white cow with a white calf at her foot is auspicious, gives one fame, and preserves life; the blessings of venerable Brahmins, well propitiated, have the same effect.

There are also some *shlokas* in conclusion :

Thus have I written in brief the Science of Love, after reading the texts of ancient authors, and following the ways of enjoyment mentioned in them.

He who is acquainted with the true principles of this science pays regard to dharma, artha, kama, *and to his own experiences, as well as to the teachings of others, and does not act simply on the dictates of his own desire. As for the unhealthy practices in the science of love which I have mentioned in this work, on my own authority as an author, I have immediately after mentioning them, carefully censured and prohibited them.*

An act is never looked upon with indulgence for the simple reason that it is authorized by the science, because it ought to be remembered that it is the intention of the science that the rules which it contains should only be acted upon in particular cases. After reading and considering the works of Babhravya and other ancient authors, and thinking over the meaning of the rules given by them, the Kama Sutra was composed, according to the precepts of the Holy Writ, for the benefit of the world, by Vatsyayana, while leading the life of a religious student, and wholly engaged in the contemplation of the Deity.

Parvati strikes a seductive pose. Ninth century, gilt-copper sculpture. (Left) A lady in a jungle skirt charms the snakes out of the trees. The cult of snake worship is integral to India.

This work is not intended to be used merely as an instrument for satisfying our desires. A person, acquainted with the true principles of this science, and who preserves his dharma, artha, *and* kama, *and has regard for the practices of the people, is sure to obtain mastery over his senses.*

In short, an intelligent and prudent person, attending to dharma *and* artha, *and attending to* kama *also, without becoming the slave of his passions, obtains success in everything that he may undertake.*

ACKNOWLEDGEMENTS

The Editor and the Publisher of Brijbasi Art Press Ltd. would like to thank the collectors for the generous use of the photographs of the unique paintings and pieces of sculpture reproduced in this book.

In particular, they wish to express their gratitude to Madame Florence, M. de Surmont, Shri J. P. Goenka, Rt. Hon. David Salman, Suresh K. Neotia, Gaylord Hoftizer, Michael Postel, Mrs Fiammeta Rossi, Mrs Sunita Pitamber, Gurappa Shetty, late David Abraham, Volkar Schafer & Michael Suessur, N. Boman Behram (heirs), Shailender M. Hem Chand, Mrs Anjolie Ella Menon, Anna Maria John, David Murdant May, Dr Daljeet Singh, Yannis Sarzetakis, Prof. Klaus Schleusener, Dr Peter Berghaus, Geo P. Bickford, late D. Langhammer.

Due recognition also goes out to the Archaeological Survey of India, New Delhi; Departments of Archaeology of the State Governments of Karnataka, Kolkata, Madhya Pradesh, Maharashtra; The National Museum, New Delhi; The Indian Museum, Kolkata; Bharat Kala Bhavan, Varanasi; Meenakshi Temple Museum, Madurai; the museums of Kabul, Afghanistan; Lahore, Pakistan; Mathura; Govt. Museums of Chandigarh, Gwalior, Chennai; the Ashutosh Museum, University of Kolkata (Prof. D. P. Ghosh); the M. C. Mehta Collection, Ahmedabad, the Dacca Museum, Bangla Desh.

The photographic archives of L. S. D. G. (Lance Dane & Satish Gupta) are the main source of the photographs reproduced here. If there is any change in the present location of any of the images, they would be pleased to revise the due recognition.